che
guevara
symbol of struggle
by tony saunois

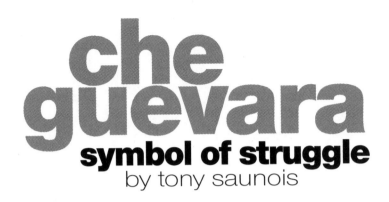

che guevara
symbol of struggle
by tony saunois

published by CWI Publications & Socialist Books

September 2005

Che Guevara
Symbol of Struggle
by Tony Saunois
© CWI Publications & Socialist Books 2005

Second Edition September 2005

ISBN 1-870958 34 9 pbk

Published by CWI Publications and Socialist Books
for the Committee for a Workers International
Designed and typeset by Kavita Graphics
Typeset in Utopia 9 pt
Printed by Russell Press (Nottingham)

Distribution by Socialist Books
PO Box 24697, London, E11 1YD
Telephone +44 (0)20 8988 8789

typesetting & design: dennis@kavitagraphics.co.uk

che guevara
symbol of struggle
by tony saunois

Forward to this edition	1
Introduction	5
A Bohemian Beginning	11
In Bolivia	19
What do I Join?	25
Guerrillaism & Marxism	33
Granma & The July 26th Movement	39
In Power: Cuba Versus the 'Gringos'	55
A New Cuba	63
Congo to Bolivia	75
Epilogue	81
Other Publications / Contacting the CWI	88

Forward
to this edition

ince this book was first published in 1997 to commemorate the thirtieth anniversary of the death of Che Guevara the political and social situation in Latin America has been transformed. Neo-liberal policies of budget cuts and privatisation have been a disaster for the entire continent. The masses of Latin America were the first suffer these polices which have now been applied on all continents by the imperialist powers and capitalism. The devastating poverty and deprivation that these policies and the continuation of capitalism cause have driven the masses throughout Latin America to fight against them. It is now a continent in revolt against neo-liberalism and even capitalism.

In this context the republication of *Che Guevara – Symbol of Struggle* and the issues discussed in it are in many respects more relevant today than when it was first published. Certainly the legacy left by Che has lived on and re-emerged during many of the recent struggles. In Santiago, Chile, when an estimated one million attended the funeral of the Chilean Communist Party leader, Gladys Marín, young people lined the streets with photos of Che. In the World Social Forum held in Brazil in 2005 placards and red flags with the emblem of Che were carried by thousands. His image has been carried on the massive demonstrations during the uprisings which took place in Ecuador and then Bolivia this year. There can be no doubt that he remains a revolutionary symbol of struggle and a source of inspiration for a new generation which has now joined the movements against capitalist and imperialist exploitation.

The revolt which is sweeping Latin America has been reflected in two clear rhythms of struggle both of which reflect the opposition of the masses to neo-liberal policies and the consequences of capitalism. Firstly, in election after election the traditional old ruling capitalist parties have been thrown out of office. A series of 'left' governments have been elected to power. In Brazil the leader of the PT (Workers' Party), Lula da Silva, was elected president for the first time. In Uruguay, Tabaré Vázquez, has become the first 'leftwing' president to be elected in the 174 year history of the country. These two 'left' presidents joined Néstor Kirchner in Argentina and Ricardo Lagos in Chile and were heralded as a 'left' wave sweeping the continent. The most radical of them is undoubtedly Hugo Chávez in Venezuela who was elected by a massive majority in 1998.

The election of these and others was greeted with massive enthusiasm by workers and the poor throughout the continent. The masses voted for these new governments with the expectation that neo-liberal policies would stop and that radical measures would be taken to end the growing poverty and social deprivation. Hopes were raised that things would now change. However, with the exception of Chávez in Venezuela, these new 'left' governments completely capitulated to imperialism and capitalism and proceeded to carry on with the same pro-capitalist policies. Privatisation continued, albeit at a slower pace, budgets were cut and the hated foreign debt continued to be paid as agreements were reached with the IMF and World Bank.

At the same time in other countries, among the most down trodden and poorest in the region, the anger has reached boiling point. Massive protests and uprisings rocked Ecuador and Bolivia. In Bolivia tens of thousands marched demanding the nationalisation of the country's energy resources which are being plundered by multi-national companies. In both cases the president was overthrown and for a brief moment important elements of power began to pass into the hands of the masses. However, despite the heroic efforts of the workers, peasants and others exploited by capitalism the opportunities were not taken and the leaders sought the route of compromise with the ruling class and allowed capitalism to continue its bloody rule through different representatives.

The capitulation to capitalism and imperialism by Lula in Brazil and other 'left' governments on the continent has not stopped the struggle against neo-liberalism and capitalism. It has now begun to take it onto a higher level. Engulfed in a massive corruption scandal Lula's government has plunged into its deepest crisis since coming to power. The pro-capitalist policies of the government have given birth to a new party, P-SOL (Party of Socialism and Liberty), which at its foundation meeting agreed to support a struggle for socialism as an alternative to capitalism. This new growing party represents an important step forward for the masses of Brazil and is an example of what is needed in other countries. If P-SOL develops and defends a programme that can seriously challenge capitalism it can become a crucial instrument in the hands of the working class and peasants to struggle for socialism.

In Bolivia and Ecuador the crisis continues and further struggles are certain to emerge in the near future.

However, in Venezuela a crucial struggle between revolution and counter-revolution is still being fought. The populist reformist government of Hugo Chávez has illustrated the new phase of the fight against capitalism which has now opened on the continent. Events in Venezuela have already had an important impact on the rest of the continent. Chávez has embarked on a programme of radical reform. His government has provoked reaction to try and overthrow it on at least three occasions. It remains a source of great irritation to US imperialism. The attempts of counter-revolution have been defeated so far by the tremendous spontaneous movements of the poor and downtrodden in Venezuela. As this struggle has developed the question of socialism has emerged once again.

Now the debate in Venezuela has turned to the question of socialism or capitalism. This, together with the other developments on the continent, represent a crucial new phase in the situation compared with the 1990s. In that decade, following the restoration of capitalism in the former USSR and Eastern Europe, the idea of socialism as an alternative to capitalism suffered a setback. However, as the Committee for a Workers' International (CWI) explained at the time, the question of socialism would emerge again as the crisis of capitalism deepened and the struggles óf working class intensified. This is now beginning to take place in Latin America. It is an anticipation of what will also develop on other continents.

These developments in Venezuela represent an important step forward and have been fully analysed in other articles and pamphlets produced by the CWI. However, the threat of reaction has not ended. Unfortunately, although now defending the idea of socialism Chávez does not advocate a programme that will break with capitalism. In Venezuela it is urgent that the working class embraces not only the idea of socialism but a programme to take power and overthrow capitalism. If this is not done then reaction will strike again and again until it succeeds in removing the Chávez government.

The ruling class in Venezuela remains fearful of the mass movement around Chávez and still wants to remove his government. Above all US imperialism wants a 'safe pair of hands' on the oil wells and regards Chávez as a serious irritant and 'destabilising factor' in the region.

An important issue is the regional role of Chávez and his proposal to supply cheap oil to other Caribbean and Latin American countries. This has been an important question for Cuba which has negotiated an agreement with Chávez in return for sending 15,000 doctors and other aid to Venezuela. Since this book was written the situation facing Fidel Castro's Cuba has also changed somewhat. Although the main questions raised about the future of Cuba in chapter nine retain there validity

Further analysis and study of the Cuban revolution and Cuba today will be found in the excellent book *Cuba – Socialism and Democracy* by Peter Taaffee which was published by the CWI in 2000.

Recently, Castro has been able to recentralise the economy and reverse some of the steps taken which began to open the economy to foreign enterprises, investment and a partial dollarisation. The oil agreement with Chávez may have given some economic benefits to Cuba but it has not enabled it to solve the chronic economic crisis which exists. Power cuts and water shortages are the latest manifestation of the crisis which exists. This crisis has provoked some anti-Castro protests.

With an ailing leader in Fidel Castro, who is now 79, the prospects for Cuba and the threat of capitalist restoration in the post-Fidel era are not fully developed in this book and are the subject of further material and analysis.

However, the stormy events in Venezuela and its links with Cuba pose the need, if the threat of capitalist restoration is to be defeated, not only for a trade agreement between the two countries. If capitalism was overthrown in Venezuela and a social-ist workers' and peasants' government was established together with a genuine workers' democracy in Cuba then a Democratic Socialist Federation of Venezuela and Cuba could be established. This could allow both economies to be planned and become a basis to extend the revolution throughout Latin America. This is the way to defeat capitalism and imperialism and the threat of counter-revolution.

These struggles in Latin America and others are fully analysed in the material of the CWI, published on our website and in other material produced by us and our affiliated sections.

It is in this context, of a new phase of struggle in Latin America, that this book about the life and ideas of Che Guevara is republished. Although the guerrillaism defended by Guevara has not yet re-emerged in most countries (it may do in some in the future) the question of the role of the working class and what programme is needed, which formed a central part of the issues discussed in this book, are more relevant than ever.

Che Guevara is still seen as a symbol of struggle by a new generation of young people in Latin America and throughout the world. Hopefully the republication of this book will assist readers to draw the necessary conclusions about the programme, strategy and tasks necessary to fight for socialism and defeat imperial-ism and capitalism.

Tony Saunois August 2005

Introduction

DURING 1996 and 1997 numerous books, pamphlets and articles have been published by assorted writers about Ernesto Guevara to commemorate the thirtieth anniversary of his execution. Throughout the world he is known simply as 'Che'. He was given this nickname by friends and comrades in struggle when he was in Mexico during the 1950s. Che is a commonly used term in Argentina - his native country. In 1997 young people in Latin America and Europe have begun to wear Che Guevara T-shirts and display posters of his portrait.

Some cynical and superficial pro-capitalist journalists attempt to dismiss the reawakened interest in Che. They falsely portray it as nothing more than a desire to be identified with the so-called permissive lifestyle associated with the 1960s.

Che Guevara undoubtedly has a romantic and cultural appeal to many young people who associate with his image as a 'rebel'.

More importantly the renewed interest in Che Guevara reflects the appeal he always had for those looking for a way to change society and end the exploitation of capitalism and imperialism. Che and Cuba are seen by many as a symbol of resistance. Reflected in the public display of support for Che Guevara by a new generation is the beginning of a search for revolutionary socialist ideas which offer a viable alternative society to capitalism.

So why has the CWI produced another pamphlet on Che and Cuba when so much has already been written on them internationally?

Apart from the cynical articles and on occasion flippant articles in some magazines and papers some serious books and biographies have already been produced. *Che Guevara - A Revolutionary Life*, by the US journalist and writer, Jon Lee Anderson, is a well researched and enjoyable biography. So is *Ernesto Guevara tambien conocido como El Che* (Ernesto Guevara also know as El Che) by the Mexican writer, Paco Ignacio Taibo (available only in Spanish).

Despite the extensive research and investigation such authors have undertaken, their work inevitably lacks one thing. They do not draw a political balance sheet of the lessons of Che's contribution to the revolutionary movement which can assist the struggle against capitalism and imperialism today. Such authors, although making a valuable contribution in recording history, cannot achieve this task. The reason is simple enough. They are not active participants in the struggle to

Che Guevara and Fidel Castro

overthrow capitalism and begin the task of building socialism.

The CWI has produced this pamphlet on Che and the 1959 Cuban revolution in order to assist in the task of building an international revolutionary socialist organisation which will be able to defeat capitalism and imperialism. History never repeats itself in exactly the same way. However, there are important lessons from previous struggles and revolutions which must be drawn by those fighting for socialism today if we are to be successful.

It is for this reason that this pamphlet has been published at this time. The Cuban revolution, in particular the contribution to it made by Che Guevara, has many lessons for the struggle against exploitation which is taking place today, especially in Latin America, Africa, Asia and the Middle East.

In order to make such a balance sheet it is necessary not only to follow the historical events which took place but to discuss the ideas and methods advocated by the central figures involved. This pamphlet is a contribution to a discussion on the experiences, ideas and methods of struggle which developed during the revolution in which Che played a principal role.

Consequently this pamphlet does not aspire to be a full personal biography of Che's life. Many aspects of his life, including his two marriages, are not covered although such personal questions are important features in the formation of any character and had a bearing on his political evolution. Neither has it been possible to give a full account of all the historical events which took place and in which Che participated. Readers will need to study other biographies and works on Cuba, Che and the Cuban revolution in order get such information.

On the thirtieth anniversary of his death it is right to recall the heroic and self-sacrificing struggle which Che conducted in opposition to capitalism and imperialism. He was a bitter opponent of capitalist exploitation and fought against it. He was drawn towards socialism largely as the result of his own experiences and was motivated by a desire to see its victory internationally. Initially he looked to the USSR (the former Soviet Union) and Eastern Europe as alternative socialist societies. This he did from 'a distance'. Later his first hand experience of those bureaucratic regimes which ruled in the name of socialism repelled him.

Committed to the life of a revolutionary by his mid-twenties, the struggle for the international revolution would cost him his life at the age of 39. He led by example and was an incorruptible internationalist. Because of these qualities he continues to be a source of inspiration as a symbol of struggle against oppression and exploitation.

Guerrillaism

At the same time his ideas were not fully rounded-out from the point of view of a full understanding of Marxism. It was his ideas on guerrillaism which had a decisive bearing on the Cuban revolution and events which followed, especially in Latin America. His defence of these ideas as a method of struggle to be adopted throughout Latin America put them at the centre of a debate in the revolutionary socialist movement throughout that continent and beyond. These ideas are discussed in this pamphlet as they have many important lessons for today's struggle against capitalism and imperialism.

Che also developed other ideas relating to the economy and what he called "socialism and the new man", which centred on how people's attitudes towards society could be developed after the overthrow of capitalism. These works reflect some of the issues he had to deal with after the revolution had taken place in 1959. Because of limitations of space it has not been possible to discuss them in this pamphlet.

A study of Che's life shows that his ideas developed over a lengthy period of time, often as the result of his own experience. He died at the relatively young age of 39. It is clear that he was still developing his ideas at the time of his death. In this respect a certain parallel exists between Che and Malcolm X and George Jackson in the USA.

Confronted by the difficulties of the situation in Cuba and the horrors he witnessed as a result of his visits behind the 'iron curtain' to the USSR and Eastern Europe, he seemed to be searching for an alternative and began to explore other ideas. He started to read some writings of Leon Trotsky a few years prior to his death. We can only speculatively pose the question: if he had continued his studies of Trotsky's ideas would he have embraced them?

In 1964 he was in Moscow to attend the celebrations for the 47th anniversary of the Russian revolution. During this visit he not only protested about the lifestyle of the Russian officials but argued that economically "... the soviets are in an economic dead-end, dominated by bureaucracy".

The bureaucratic caste in China at this time was presenting a more 'radical face' internationally in an effort to win support after the rupture which had taken place between it and the USSR bureaucracy. This had occurred as a result of a clash of narrow national interests between the two regimes.

Che was attracted towards the Chinese bureaucracy as a result of the 'radical face' it presented during this period and also because of the victory of the peasant army which had taken place in 1949. It appeared to confirm his own analysis. However, he also began to explore the ideas of Leon Trotsky. In Moscow he was attacked as being "pro-Chinese" and a "Trotskyist". Aware of these denunciations Che referred to them in a meeting in the Cuban embassy with Cuban students. The incident is recounted in Paco Ignacio Taibo's biography.

Che commented: *"... I have expressed opinions which could be closer to the Chinese side... and also those mixed up with Trotskyism have come up. They say that the Chinese are fractionalists, also the Trotskyists and me as well."* He continued: *"Opinion which must be destroyed with batons is opinion which brings us an advantage. It is not possible to destroy opinions with batons and it is precisely this that is the root of intelligence... it is clear that you can get a series of things from Trotsky's thought."*

Trotskyism

There is no indication of what conclusions Che was drawing from any reading of Trotsky's writings and he did not advocate ideas which would have flowed from him embracing Trotskyism. However, he did continue to study them further. Just before his death in 1967 he was given some books of Trotsky by the French intellectual, Regis Debray, who was in Bolivia, working with Guevara's forces at the time.

During this period the dominant current which subscribed to Trotskyism (the United Secretariat of the Fourth International, USFI, led by Ernest Mandel) failed to engage in an open political dialogue and discussion with a view to helping Che develop fully rounded-out ideas on the socialist revolution.It merely supported and encouraged the ideas on guerrillaism which he advocated and gave support to Fidel Castro's regime.

This was combated at the time by some within the Trotskyist movement, including the then tiny forces in Britain organised in Militant (now the Socialist Party) who later established the Committee for a Workers' International (CWI). In 1960 at the time of the stormy events in Cuba the members of Militant enthusiastically welcomed the revolution and the overthrow of Fulgencio Batista but also explained the character of the new regime which developed and the need to look to the working class in order to develop the revolution throughout Latin America.

Later, Peter Taaffe, in an article in Issue 390 of the British *Militant* newspaper explained the processes which had unfolded in Cuba: "Castro and Guevara relied on the peasants and the rural population. The working class only entered the struggle through the general strike in Havana when the guerrillas had already triumphed and Batista was fleeing for his life." Explaining how this rural base shaped the whole character of the movement, he continued to outline how the revolution unfolded, ending in the abolition of capitalism and private ownership of land by the big landowners but, "because of the forces involved - a predominantly peasant army", the new regime lacked conscious democratic control and management of the economy by the working class.

Despite encountering some of Trotsky's ideas in his search for an alternative, Che unfortunately did not embrace the alternative ideas or methods of Trotskyism. Nevertheless his actions were sufficient to provoke a reaction in the Kremlin and elsewhere. In Cuba and amongst the Latin American masses Che was a hero whose revolutionary example should be emulated. Amongst the ruling circles of the

Sierra Maestra Mountains, early 1957

bureaucracy in Moscow he was attacked as 'an adventurer' 'pro-Chinese' and worst of all a 'Trotskyist'. The ruling class of the capitalist countries hated everything he defended and fought for.

Che was executed by those people intent on defending the rich and powerful. His image lives on as a symbol of struggle against oppression. As protests against 'neo-liberal' policies and the market have erupted in Latin America it is still common to find graffiti scribbled on walls by young people: "Che -Vive" - Che Lives.

To commemorate the anniversary of his execution it is justified that those fighting capitalist exploitation internationally should learn important lessons from his ideas and experiences in order to win the victory he desired - socialism. This pamphlet is intended as a contribution to assist in that struggle.

Tony Saunois September 1997

A Bohemian Beginning

I T IS perhaps fitting for an Argentinean to own a yerba mate plantation as Ernesto Guevara Lynch did in the remote jungle of Misiones on the border with Paraguay and Brazil. Chileans are renowned drinkers of tea and Brazilians of coffee. The Argentineans consume with gusto a bitter tea herb, 'mate', throughout the day whilst at work or relaxing with friends.

Ernesto Guevara Lynch was the great-grandson of one of South America's richest men whose ancestors were of both Spanish and Irish nobility. Most of the family fortune had been lost by previous generations and Guevara Lynch invested what he had in the yerba mate plantation where he hoped to make his fortune. In 1927 he met and married Celia de la Serna, an Argentinean also with ancestors from the Spanish nobility.

The first of four children, Ernesto, was to become known as the world renowned revolutionary, Che Guevara. As a revolutionary who spent most of his life in clandestine activity, it was apt that he should have falsified birth and death certificates.

Ernesto was in fact born one month earlier than 14 June 1928 which was stated on his birth certificate, the deception being necessary because his mother was three months pregnant on the day she married. Che was executed on 8 October 1967 in Bolivia at the hands of the US Central Intelligence Agency (CIA) and the Bolivian army.

Thirty years after his execution the name of Che Guevara lives on throughout Latin America and beyond. He has left a powerful tradition as an internationalist and self-sacrificing revolutionary who acts as an inspiring symbol of struggle against exploitation.

On the thirtieth anniversary of his execution it is legitimate for revolutionaries to salute Che's qualities as a symbol of struggle against oppression and recognise the heroic role he played in the Cuban revolution in 1959. The guerrilla struggle which was mainly based upon the most downtrodden peasants in Cuba ended with the overthrow of the hated Batista dictatorship.

This was possible because of the concrete situation which existed in Cuba and other countries of Central America and the Caribbean. It was not possible for Che to successfully repeat the experience of the revolution in the countries of Latin

America where there were different conditions - in particular a more powerful urban population and smaller rural population than in Central America.

The attempt of Che to apply the same methods he used in Cuba poses important questions about his ideas and methods which need to be discussed and analysed by revolutionary socialists.

Upbringing

Che did not readily enter into political activity. Reflecting his middle class upbringing and compassion for the poor and sick he was initially drawn towards medicine and eventually graduated as a doctor from the Buenos Aires Faculty of Medicine in 1953.

His family had moved from Misiones to Cordoba partly for business reasons and also in a bid to aid Che's chronic asthma through a change of climate. They finally moved to Buenos Aires in 1947 where his parents eventually split up.

Asthma was to dog Che throughout his life. Its crippling effects made all the more remarkable the guerrilla struggles which he eventually was to engage in. Like many such disabilities it shaped his early development. Often unable to walk and confined to bed he developed a keen interest in reading and learning to play chess. Whilst determined to overcome his disability and insisting on playing sports he became something of a loner spending much of his time reading and studying. This was reinforced by the split between his parents, the death of his grandmother and the financial problems which the family were now encountering.

At university Che was drawn to more political reading although he did not actively participate in political life. He began delving into socialist ideas. According to his own recollections he read some Karl Marx, Frederich Engels and Vladimir Lenin along with some material by Joseph Stalin. He also studied the novelists Emile Zola and Jack London and Argentine socialists such as Alfredo Palacios. His love of poetry was satisfied, amongst others, by the works of the Chilean writer and Communist Party member, Pablo Neruda, and the Spanish Civil War poet Frederico Lorca.

However, for all his new-found curiosity about socialist ideas he never engaged in political activity beyond discussing with some members of the Young Communists and other left-wing groups. According to one report he joined the Peronist Youth (a populist and nationalist Argentinean movement led by General Juan Perón) as a means of obtaining greater access to the university library.

He was regarded as radical and outspoken by those he encountered but did not have any coherent or worked out ideas and certainly did not regard himself as a Marxist. His main objective was still to qualify as a doctor with a view to helping the sick and the poor. However, within him a passion for travel was beginning to develop. Initially this was within Argentina itself and then later he undertook two journeys which brought him throughout Latin America and eventually beyond.

Journeys of discovery

The experiences which he encountered during this odyssey changed his perception of the tasks necessary to end poverty and exploitation. It was during the adventures and events which he witnessed on these journeys that Che eventually embraced socialist ideas.

Che's first real journey took place during 1950 when he travelled widely throughout Argentina. For the first time he witnessed the massive social divide which existed in the country. In Buenos Aires he had evidently seen poverty before but for the first time he witnessed the dual character of much of South America. Buenos Aires was one of the most European of South American cities in its culture and lifestyle. During this journey he travelled into the backward and socially deprived centres of Argentina which existed at the time.

Much of what he saw in the hospitals he visited and amongst the most downtrodden of the rural poor with which he made contact was viewed through the eyes of an aspiring doctor. Che concluded from these experiences that the modern Argentinean nation was a 'luxurious façade' under which the real 'soul' lay, a soul which was rotten and sick.

Che's first international tour took place in 1952 and the second during 1953/4. These had a more pronounced effect and ultimately changed the direction of his entire life, especially his second odyssey throughout the continent.

Nobody can escape the consequences of powerful social upheavals and convulsions. It is true that some individuals, especially from a middle class background, may be content to only observe such events. Others are increasingly drawn into big social events and the struggles between the various classes. Che Guevara was content to play the role of an observer at the beginning of his voyage. As it progressed he was increasingly drawn into the revolutionary struggle which ultimately cost him his life.

At the outset of his voyage he and his travelling companion, Alberto Granado, were more interested in having a good time and gaining some medical experience as they toured South America on a Harley Davidson. Che's Motor Cycle Diaries provide more than adequate examples of this. Drunken brawls, romantic encounters and other, 'youthful' adventures, dominated the trip they were making around the continent. As they crossed the border into Chile they passed themselves off as leprologists. The local papers of the towns and villages they passed through even reported the journey of these two young adventurers. The local daily in Temuco carried the headline 'Two Argentine Experts in Leprology Travel South America on a

Motor Cycle.'

Frequently they had to flee local towns and villages having aroused the wrath of the local peasants, especially fathers with attractive daughters. During this first trip Che led the largely bohemian and carefree existence for which he was known as a student at university in Buenos Aires. It was a lifestyle made all the more possible by the relative affluence of his middle class family. At the same time it also reflected the independent spirit which marked his character.

However, whilst it is this aspect of the trip which is the dominant feature in his diary, other experiences had an important impact on him. The poverty and conditions he witnessed increasingly aroused a nascent social awareness. Che's anger at the indifference shown towards the poor by the ruling class was being stirred during his travels.

Whilst encamped at the Chilean port of Valparaíso, Che was asked to use his medical skills to try and help an elderly woman who it transpired was dying of chronic asthma and a weak heart. There was little he could do but the experience of trying to treat her, surrounded by poverty, evidently lefts its mark. Afterwards he wrote: *"There, in the final moments of people whose farthest horizon is always tomorrow, one sees the tragedy that enfolds the lives of the proletariat throughout the whole world; in those dying eyes there is a submissive apology and also, frequently, a desperate plea for consolation that is lost in the void, just as their body will soon be lost in the magnitude of misery surrounding us. How long this order of things based on an absurd sense of caste will continue is not within my means to answer, but it is time that those who govern dedicate less time to propagandising the compassion of their regimes and more money, much more money, sponsoring works of social utility."*

Miners' Struggle

Unable to get a boat to Easter Island as they intended Che and his companion headed north, eventually arriving at Chuquicamata, the world's largest open-cast copper mine. 'Chuqui', as it is still known in Chile today, was owned by US monopolies such as Anaconda and Kennecott. US ownership of the mines at 'Chuqui' was a symbol of imperialist 'gringo' domination of Chile. They were eventually nationalised by the Popular Unity government, led by Salvador Allende of the Socialist Party, between 1970 and 1973.

It was here that Che and Alberto encountered the harsh realities of the class struggle. They met a former miner and his wife, both members of the then illegal Chilean Communist Party. Che was told the bitter story of repression, disappearances and blacklisting used by the company and government against those who tried to fight for workers' rights.

Che and Alberto succeeded in entering the mine where a strike was being prepared. They were shown around by a foreman who, as Che noted, commented, *"... imbecile gringos, they lose millions of pesos a day in a strike in order to deny a few centavos more to a poor worker".*

This visit to Chuqui made a lasting impression on Che and he kept a notebook on the experience in which he detailed not only the impressions he had of the workers but also production techniques and the political importance of the mines for Chile. Referring to the mineral rich mountains he protested about the "exploited proletariat" and environmental destruction of the landscape: *"The hills show their grey backs prematurely aged in the struggle against the elements, with elderly wrinkles that don't correspond to their geological age. How many of these escorts of their famous brother (Chuquicamata) enclosed in their heavy wombs similar riches to his, as they await the arid arms of the mechanical shovels that devour their entrails, with their obligatory condiment of human lives?"* [1]

However, despite these scenes and the impact they had on Che, he would still need further experiences and witness greater events before he committed himself to the life of a revolutionary.

Inca Culture

The next stop on his odyssey was Peru which proved decisive in Che embracing socialist ideas through an encounter with a prominent leader of the Peruvian Communist Party, Doctor Hugo Pesce. Before arriving in Lima on 1 May 1952, Che and Alberto had the opportunity to encounter the marvel of ancient Inca culture.

As with all visitors, the stark consequences of four hundred years of 'white' European conquest in Latin America and brutal suppression of the indigenous peoples of the continent were undoubtedly engraved into the consciousness of Che during his visit to the ancient Inca capital of Cuzco and the stunning temple ruins of Machu Picchu.

Pablo Neruda in his celebrated work on Latin America, *Canto General* (General Song) included a poem, *Alturas de Machu Picchu* (The Heights of Machu Picchu) reflecting the image this ancient ruin high in the Andes provokes in those aspiring to struggle against exploitation:

" *Then up the ladder of the earth I climbed*
through the barbed jungle's thickets
until I reached you, Machu Picchu.

Tall city of stepped stone,
home at long last of whatever earth
had never hidden in her sleeping clothes.

In you two lineage's that had run parallel
met where the cradle both of man and light
rocked in a wind of thorns.

Mother of stone and sperm of condors.

High reef of the human dawn..."

In Che's native Argentina the indigenous peoples had been virtually wiped out and their cultures destroyed. In Peru, Bolivia, Mexico and some other Latin American countries this was not the case. They had been reduced to the most downtrodden and exploited layers of society, often predominating in the countryside. The mixed race mestizos had developed and formed big sections of the working class in the cities. The rich and powerful ruling classes were and remain largely of European descent.

This history of conquest and the continued exploitation of the continent by imperialism, especially US imperialism, has resulted in an extremely powerful anti-imperialist consciousness amongst the exploited classes. In the latter half of the 20th century and beginning of the 21st this bitterness has been largely directed at the 'yanki gringos', north of the Rio Grande. Che during his visit to Peru increasingly absorbed this hatred of the dominant imperialist power.

Upon being forced to leave the free accommodation they had secured with the arrival of a party of 'gringo' tourists, Che noted: *"Naturally the tourists who travelled in their comfortable buses would know nothing of the conditions of the Indians... The majority of the Americans fly directly from Lima to Cuzco, visit the ruins and then return, without giving any importance to anything else."*

On 1 May the two travellers arrived in Lima. Che met with Dr Pesce, a leading figure in the Communist Party and follower of the Peruvian philosopher José Maríategui. Maríategui's primary work was written in 1928 - Seven Interpretative Essays on Peruvian Reality. This laid great stress on the role of the indigenous people and peasantry in the struggle for socialism.

The discussions with Pesce evidently had a profound effect upon Che. A decade later he sent the doctor a copy of his first book, Guerrilla Warfare, with the inscription: "To Doctor Hugo Pesce who, without knowing it perhaps, provoked a great change in my attitude towards life and society, with the same adventurous spirit as always, but channelled toward goals more harmonious with the needs of America."

At this stage, despite the discussions he was engaged in with Pesce, Che was still not prepared to openly embrace 'Marxist' ideas. His opinions were however beginning to take shape and he began to express them. In particular he began to openly develop internationalist ideas, at least within the context of Latin America.

Internationalism

At a party to celebrate his twenty-fourth birthday in Peru, Che made a toast declaring "... *that [Latin] America's division into illusory and uncertain nationalities is completely fictitious. We constitute a single mestizo race, which from Mexico to the Straights of Magellan presents notable ethnographic similarities. For this, in an attempt to rid myself of the weight of any meagre provincialism, I raise a toast to Peru and for a United America.*"

This statement clearly reflected his developing internationalist aspirations. However, they did not constitute a rounded out Marxist analysis and were somewhat simplistic in the assessment of the situation. The aspiration for a unified Latin America has existed since Simón Bolívar (who led armed rebellions against Spain and helped secure independence for much of Latin America) and the 19th century wars of national liberation. Continental unity is still a powerful sentiment amongst the Latin American masses, existing side by side with a national consciousness in each country.

The recurring aspiration of the masses to unify Latin America is not possible to obtain within the context of capitalism. This is because the ruling capitalist classes of each Latin American nation have their own economic and political interests to defend. They are also linked by economic and material interests to imperialism from which they cannot break free. Imperialism itself also opposes unity of the continent under capitalism generally preferring to impose its will on a number of states weaker than itself. The establishment of a democratic federation of Latin American states as a step to unify the continent is only possible by breaking free of capitalism and imperialism and building socialism.

This spirit of internationalism was a theme to which Che returned many times and the idea of an internationally based revolution against imperialism and capitalism was one he championed in later years. The divergence he had with a fully rounded-out Marxist analysis was about how this should be done and by which class.

After continuing his tour, arriving in Colombia and Venezuela, Che, having separated from his travel companion and friend, returned to Argentina in order to complete his studies and sit exams at university. The impact of this first journey upon him was evident in his *Notas de Viaje*, written up from his travel diary. He was no longer the same person who had left Argentina: "*The person who wrote these notes died upon stepping once again onto Argentine soil, he who edits and polishes them, 'I' am not I; at least I am not the same I that was before. That vagabonding through our 'America' has changed me more than I thought.*"

Once back in Argentina his family hoped that his days as a vagabond would end and that he would take up his chosen profession, medicine. Che completed his studies during April 1953 and received his doctor's degree in June, a few days prior to his twenty fifth-birthday.

However, the hopes held by his family were rapidly dashed as his second tour of America began. This time it was planned together with his childhood friend, Carlos 'Calica' Ferrer, who had dropped out of medical school.

According to Calica, the two friends had talked of going through Bolivia to Peru as Che wanted to return to visit the Inca ruins and Machu Picchu. Their longer-term plans included Che's hopes of visiting India and Calica's quest to see Paris.

Thus by early July, when the two travel companions set off by train from Buenos Aires, Che still had no idea of committing himself to a life of disciplined and self-sacrificing revolutionary struggle. The bohemian still dominated his character. Within a relatively short space of time this was to change.

Individuals are drawn to participate in the revolutionary movement for many reasons. Some are mainly motivated by political ideas, others by revulsion of the existing system, and some through participating in big social upheavals from which they cannot simply stand aside.

The reason Che's life took a sharp turn in another direction cannot be explained by one single issue. He was undoubtedly interested in political ideas and was outraged by the social conditions which he witnessed. He was also profoundly affected by the powerful social explosions he experienced during his second American tour. These included two revolutionary movements, in Bolivia and then Guatemala, after which his life took an entirely new and unexpected direction.

1 At the time, Chile was involved in a presidential election campaign which was eventually won by the populist nationalist candidate, General Carlos Ibanez del Campo. Once in power he concluded an agreement with US imperialism and introduced a savage deflationary package which included reneging on a pledge to nationalise the copper mines at Chuqui. In the election the socialist and left-wing candidate, Salvador Allende, came last, partly due to the legal ban on the Communist Party and its supporters. Allende was eventually elected president in 1970, the first Socialist Party candidate to win a popular presidential election campaign in South America. On victory he proclaimed himself to be a Marxist. One of the first acts of this socialist-led government was to nationalise the mines at Chuqui. Allende's government was overthrown in a CIA backed bloody coup in 1973.

In Bolivia

DURING THIS second tour Che penned another journal which he entitled, *Otra Vez* (Once Again).[1] Reflecting how he began this journey he wrote: *"This time, the name of the sidekick has changed, now Alberto is called Calica, but the journey is the same: two disperse wills extending themselves through America without knowing precisely what they seek or which way is north."*

Che and companion arrived in La Paz, the Bolivian capital, during July 1953. They were immediately caught up in the revolutionary upheavals which were rocking one of the poorest and most 'Indian' of American nations. A mass revolt of the predominantly indigenous peasants and tin miners had broken out twelve months earlier. This mass uprising had brought the radical Movimiento Nacionalista Revolucionario (MNR) to power.

The new regime, whilst trying to keep the mass movement in check, was forced by the insurrectionary upheavals to carry through a widespread programme of reform. The peasants, through a series of land occupations, forced a far reaching programme of agrarian reform. The tin mines, Bolivia's primary source of income at the time, were nationalised. The miners and peasants had armed themselves; sections of the army came over to the side of the workers and peasants. A militia was established and for a short time the army was formally disbanded. However, the revolution was not completed with the establishment of a new regime of workers' democracy and the movement was eventually defeated.

During these revolutionary events the tin miners played a leading role in establishing a new independent trade union centre, the Central Obrera Boliviana (COB). Reflecting the revolutionary upsurge which took place the COB even formally endorsed the *Transitional Programme*, written by Trotsky in 1938.

In La Paz, Che spent much of his time in cafés and bars meeting political migrants who had arrived from all over America. During the course of the revolution Bolivia had become a political Mecca as radicals and left-wing revolutionaries were attracted to the stormy events erupting.

"La Paz is the Shanghai of the Americas. A rich gamut of adventurers of all the nationalities vegetate and flourish in the polychromatic and mestizo city," wrote Che in *Otra Vez*. Here he mixed with a variety of political activists and engaged in discus-

sions with them. He met up with some of the Argentine community living in La Paz. Amongst those he met was an exiled Argentinean, called Gobo Nogues.

The influence of the powerful social events taking place in Bolivia are reflected in Che's comments about this leader of the expatriate Argentinean community: *"His political ideas have been outdated in the world for some time now, but he maintains them independently of the proletarian hurricane that has been let loose on our bellicose sphere."*

Through these social contacts Che led a double existence in La Paz alternating between observing the revolutionary movements and the high life he was introduced to through the Argentine community. On one occasion, Nogues' brother, having recently returned from Europe, showed Che and Calica an invitation he had received to the wedding of Greek shipping tycoon, Aristotle Onassis.

Flames of Revolution

However, it was the revolutionary process which he witnessed in La Paz which left the most lasting impression on Che. He wrote to his father in July complaining that he wanted to stay in Bolivia longer because, *"... this is a very interesting country and it is living through a particularly effervescent moment. On the second of August the agrarian reform goes through, and fracases and fights are expected throughout the country. We have seen incredible processions of armed people with Mausers and 'piripipi' [machine guns], which they shoot off for the hell of it. Every day shots can be heard and there are wounded and dead from firearms."*

Che, who wanted to see the renowned Bolivian miners first hand, visited the Balsa Negra mine just outside La Paz. Prior to the revolution company guards had used a machine gun to open fire on striking miners. Now the mine was nationalised. Che encountered truck loads of armed miners returning from the capital to protest their support for land reform and the struggle of peasants. With their *"stony faces and red plastic helmets they appeared to be warriors from other worlds"*.

Despite witnessing the tremendous strength of the Bolivian miners Che never really absorbed the potential role of the working class in the socialist revolution, even in countries such as Bolivia where it constituted a minority of the population. This weakness combined with other factors would have a direct bearing on the ideas he later developed.

At this stage in Che's political evolution, however it is sufficient to note the impact which events in Bolivia had on his outlook. For the first time in his life he was touched directly by the heat of the flame of revolution. Despite the sweep of events he was still an observer rather than an active participant.

After extending their stay in La Paz to nearly one month Che and Calica moved on. They spent some time in Peru and in Lima again met with Doctor Pesce and also

Gobo Nogues. Gobo ensured that they ate on a few occasions at the Country Club and in Lima's most expensive hotel, the Gran Hotel Bolívar.

They moved on to Ecuador where they forged new friendships with a group of adventurers. Che's intention had been to move on with Calica to Venezuela. After a series of excursions Calica and Che departed company, the former heading for Caracas and the latter with a new companion, Gualo, to Guatemala. They were totally broke and had to work their passage on a ship. Before reaching Guatemala they passed through Costa Rica, Panama and Nicaragua, meeting and discussing with individuals and groups along the way.

By travelling north to Central America Che had entered a somewhat different world to that which existed in the southern cone of Latin America. Imperialism dominated the southern countries in conjunction with an enfeebled national capitalist class. There was a relatively strong urban population and working class in the cities and the societies tended to be more developed. This was even the case in the poorest countries at the time, such as Bolivia and Peru.

In a series of Central American countries US imperialism arrogantly imposed local tyrants as dictatorial heads of state while despised and hated companies, such as Coca Cola and the United Fruit Company, plundered the economies. As Che commented, "... the countries were not true nations, but private estancias".

This was only fifty years after US imperialism had created Panama and ran it as a client state in order to keep control of the canal which it had built for trade purposes and strategic interests. Nicaragua had been ruled for thirty years by the corrupt dictatorship of Anastasio Somoza. El Salvador was run by a succession of dictatorships intent on defending the interests of the coffee plantation owners, and Honduras was virtually run as a packaging plant for the United Fruit Company.

The United Fruit Company symbolised the exploitation of the continent by imperialism. Che's favourite poet, Pablo Neruda, wrote an ironical verse, *La United Fruit Co*, reflecting the sentiments of Latin America towards its imperialist domination:

" *When the trumpet sounded,*
everything was prepared on earth,
and Jehovah divided the world between
Coca-Cola Inc, Anaconda,
Ford Motors, and other entities:
the United Fruit Company Inc;
reserved for itself the most beautiful place,
the central coast of my land;
the sweet waist of America..."

Neruda's poem continues and denounces the company for creating the *"Tyrannical Reign of Flies"* the dictators of Central America: Trujillo, Tachos, Ubico, Martínez, Garias, *"the bloody domain of flies"*.

On to Guatemala

If events in Bolivia had made an impact on Che, developments in Guatemala, where he got actively involved for the first time, would change the direction of his life. He arrived in Guatemala City on Christmas Eve and openly identified with a political cause and with some idea of what he now intended to commit his life to.

Just prior to his arrival he had written a letter dated 10 December, in which he outlined his political views to his aunt Beatríz with whom he had an especially close relationship. These were undoubtedly a reflection of the effect events in Bolivia had on him. For the first time he clearly identified himself ideologically with socialist ideas: *"My life has been a sea of found resolutions until I bravely abandoned my baggage and, back pack on my shoulder, set out with el compañero García on the sinuous trail that has brought us here. Along the way I have had the opportunity to pass through the dominions of the United Fruit, convincing me once again of just how terrible these capitalist octopuses are. I have sworn before a picture of the old and mourned Stalin that I won't rest until I see these capitalist octopuses annihilated. In Guatemala I will perfect myself and achieve what I need to be an authentic revolutionary."* He signed the letter *"from your nephew of the iron constitution, the empty stomach and the shining faith in the socialist future. Chao, Chancho"*.

By 1953 the populist left-leaning government in Guatemala, presided over by Colonel Jacobo Arbenz, was locked into a head-on confrontation with US imperialism and the rich elite of Guatemala City. Arbenz was continuing a reformist programme begun by the preceding government which came to power during the 1940s having toppled the ruthless Ubico dictatorship.

US imperialism would tolerate a lot from this reformist administration. But in 1952 the Arbenz administration took a step too far. A land reform decree was enacted which abolished the latifundia system and nationalised the properties of the detested United Fruit Company.

This measure provoked the wrath of Guatemala's white Creole elite and won massive support from the mainly indigenous and mestizo poor rural peasants and urban workers. The United Fruit Company and Dwight Eisenhower's administration were outraged. It would only be a matter of time before the CIA would instigate the overthrow of the Arbenz government.

The 'socialist' experiment in Guatemala had drawn thousands from all over Latin America to see first hand this challenge to US imperialism. Mass mobilisations were taking place all the time and numerous militias were established by both the government and the various political parties. In the main these were not armed. However, the forces of reaction began to arm and mobilise.

 Amongst those present during the Guatemalan drama, apart from Che Guevara, were numerous future leaders of Latin American left-wing organisations, including Rodolfo Romero, a future leader of the Nicaraguan Sandinista FSLN (Frente Sandinista de Liberación Nacional) which overthrew the Somoza dictatorship in 1979.

Che met with a series of political activists and engaged in discussion. He secured work as a doctor in a hospital and was introduced to Hilda Gadea, an exiled leader of the youth wing of the radical populist Peruvian movement, APRA. She introduced him to activists and leaders of various political groupings and gave him political works to study, including some works of Mao Zedong.

It was during these events that Che encountered a number of Cuban exiles. They had been given asylum by the Arbenz regime and had participated in an attempted assault on 26 July 1953 against the Moncada military barracks in Cuba. For the first time Che began to discover about the struggle developing against the Cuban Batista regime.

The Popular Front

The speed with which events developed in Guatemala also resulted in Che's ideas maturing. He began to criticise the communist parties which had adopted a policy of 'Popular' or 'People's Fronts'. This put them in alliances with sections of the national capitalist class. The leadership of the communist parties wrongly argued that a tactical alliance with this 'progressive' wing of the national capitalist class was necessary in the struggle against imperialism in order to defend and widen parliamentary democracy. They said a stage of 'capitalist democracy and economic development' was necessary before the working class could struggle for and hope to obtain socialism.

This policy resulted in the communist party leaders limiting the struggles of the working class to prevent them challenging the interests of capitalism. The workers' movement was frequently paralysed by this policy which often resulted in bloody defeat at the hands of reaction. Decisive sections of the capitalist class were quite prepared to abolish democratic rights and utilise repressive methods of rule in order to defend their own class interests.

Che, although not clearly presenting an alternative to this policy, felt that the communist parties were moving away from the masses simply to get a share of power in coalition governments. He wrongly argued at this time that no party in Latin America could remain revolutionary and contest elections.

Though beginning to articulate his thoughts, Che's ideas did not become fully formulated until later. Meanwhile events in Guatemala overtook the polemics he had begun to be engaged in. The US was increasingly uneasy about the course events were taking and had concluded that the government must be overthrown. The example of the movement in Guatemala was beginning to spill over into other Central American countries. A general strike broke out in Honduras. The Nicaraguan dictator, Somoza, feared his own population may follow the example of events in neighbouring countries.

The CIA had put together a plan to topple the Guatemalan administration. A figurehead named Castillo Armas was hand-picked to replace Arbenz as President. A paramilitary force was trained in Nicaragua and those friendly to the US in the Guatemalan army were involved in a plot against the government.

Arbenz refused to take action against those in the military known to be sympathetic to the plotters and tried to appease the military. A few days before his government was overthrown in 1954 by the conspirators he appealed to the army itself to distribute arms to the militias which had been established. The military command refused and the government fell. The existing capitalist state machine had been left intact and no alternative of workers' and peasants' committees had been established from which an appeal could have been made to the rank-and-file soldiers.

This defeat and the failure of Arbenz to take any action against the capitalist state apparatus were to leave a lasting impression on Che, one which he would not forget as the revolution in Cuba unfolded.

After seeking asylum in the Argentinean embassy and hiding for a period, Che eventually found his way to Mexico by September. As a fresh activist his movements had not gone unnoticed. The CIA opened a file on him for the first time. Over the coming years it was to become one of the thickest ever compiled by them on any one individual.

It was while Che was in Mexico that he initially met one of the leaders of the July 26th Movement fighting the Batista dictatorship in Cuba, Fidel Castro. Their first meeting was during 1955, after which Che eventually joined the Movement.

Following his experiences in Bolivia and in particular after his participation in events in Guatemala, Che entered the next phase of his life no longer as the medical doctor and social observer. From this point on he was to be an active participant in and eventual leader of historic events.

2 This journal, covering three years of Che's life has never been fully published. It was transcribed by his widow, Aleida March, after Che's death. It was made available to the writer Jon Lee Anderson and extensively used by him in his celebrated biography, Che Guevara - A Revolutionary Life, published in 1997.

What do I Join?

BY THE time Che had arrived in Mexico his open commitment to socialism had been strengthened. Whilst in Mexico he developed his studies of Marx, Engels and Lenin and supplemented them with further reading of London and other writers. However, despite the evolution of Che's political knowledge, his grasp of Marxist theory was still one-sided and incomplete.

This weakness was particularly evident in his interpretation of how to apply a Marxist method to the colonial and semi-colonial countries of Latin America. This would become clear in a very real way as he engaged in the concrete struggle to overthrow the Batista dictatorship in Cuba.

Che was drawn to the July 26th Movement which was initiated by Fidel Castro rather than the Cuban Communist Party. This decision has puzzled many on the left especially in Latin America. The answer lies in the role and policies advocated by the communist parties throughout Latin America at that time and the character of the July 26th Movement.

The July 26th Movement was so named to commemorate the date of an assault on the Moncada military barracks in the Cuban city of Santiago during 1953. This attack was carried out by a group of youth who were mainly linked with the Cuban People's Party (Partido del Pueblo Cubano), known as the Orthodox Party. This was a radical Cuban nationalist formation which had split from the Auténticos (Authentic Revolutionary Movement) in 1947 and was led by Eduardo Chibas whose main programme was "honesty in government". The Auténticos, reorganised during the 1930s, initially attempted to lay claim to the 19th century national democratic revolutionary tradition of Cuba's national hero, José Martí - the poet and fighter for independence who was killed in 1895 whilst leading a charge on horseback against the Spanish army.

Martí and the independence movement were comprised of many strands and included a certain anarchist influence from the growing Spanish workers' movement. Martí himself supported a radical social programme. He was influenced by certain anarchist organisations which had links with the Spanish workers' movement. However, as Hugh Thomas points out in his extensive tome, *Cuba - The Pursuit of Freedom*, Martí "... *from his writings, seems a contemporary of Rousseau rather than of Marx..."* Martí was in essence a fighter for national independence and defender of 'social justice'. He did not however advocate a break with capitalism or defend socialist ideas.

The Auténticos increasingly modified their stand just as the Orthodox Party was destined to do less than a decade later. Within the youth wing of the Orthodox Party a radical current was to be found which increasingly became frustrated by the lack of serious struggle by the party against the Batista regime.

Those who carried out the attack on the Moncada barracks hoped that it would begin a national uprising. Instead it was brutally crushed and its participants either killed or imprisoned. Amongst those involved in the assault were Fidel Castro and his brother Raúl. Most of the 170 participants were either from a lower middle class or working class background. Despite this they were not advocates of socialist ideas. Raúl Castro was a member of the Young Communists but had participated in the attack as an individual and without the knowledge of the Communist Party.

Insugents' Programme

The majority were not members of any political organisation. The programme they advocated was mainly limited to the radical aspects of the policy of the democratic but capitalist Orthodox Party. Fidel Castro was no exception. At that stage he did not regard himself as a socialist and he was certainly not committed to Marxist ideology despite having read some Marx and Lenin.

The basic idea which the insurgents at Moncada advocated can be gauged from the proclamation they read after the capture of the radio station: *"The Revolution declares its firm intention to establish Cuba on a plan of welfare and economic prosperity that ensures the survival of its rich subsoil, its geographical position, diversified agriculture and industrialisation... The Revolution declares its respect for the workers... and... the establishment of total and definitive social justice, based on economic and industrial progress under a well organised and timed national plan..."* The proclamation affirmed that it *"... recognises and bases itself upon the ideas of Martí"*, and then pledged itself to restore the constitution of 1940.

In other words it proposed a programme to established in Cuba a modern, industrialised capitalist democracy which would grant elementary rights to the working class and the poor. This was amplified still further by Castro after his arrest in the speech he delivered during his trial. Castro outlined five laws they intended to implement once in power. These were radical and promised nationalisation of the telephone system and other public utilities, a programme of land reform and proposals to restructure the sugar industry. It proposed a profit sharing scheme in the sugar mills and other non-agricultural sectors of the economy.

However, the programme did not even propose the nationalisation of the sugar industry and would not have ended foreign ownership of the economy. In essence it was a programme of liberal capitalist reform which if implemented would attempt to tackle the tasks of the bourgeois democratic revolution.

Historically, these tasks include a programme of land reform to end feudal class relations, the development of industry, the unification of the country into a nation state, the establishment of capitalist parliamentary democracy and the winning of national independence from imperialist domination laying the basis for the modern nation state.

The exact form the tasks of the bourgeois democratic revolution takes differs from country to country. In certain countries some of the questions posed can be resolved or partly resolved while others remain to be achieved. For example in Argentina capitalist property relations as opposed to feudal ownership exists in the rural areas. However, Argentina is still shackled by the domination of the major imperialist countries' economic power.

In the semi-colonial and colonial countries such as Cuba implementing the programme of the democratic bourgeois revolution has meant a conflict with capitalism and imperialism. This is because the national capitalist class is too weak -linked to the landowners and shackled to imperialism- to accomplish the bourgeois democratic revolution. A further factor is the fear the national bourgeoisie has of the working class entering any arena of struggle against imperialism.

The vice in which Cuba was locked by imperialism, together with the decadent Cuban ruling class, was too strong to permit even a limited programme of liberal reform. As in other non-industrialised countries, the national capitalist class in Cuba was too weak, corrupt and shackled to imperialism to complete the tasks of the bourgeois democratic revolution. And yet these tasks need to be resolved if society is to develop.

As the Russian revolution had illustrated in 1917 this dilemma could be solved only by the working class, even in a country where it was in a minority. It could do this by taking control of the running of society and establishing a workers' democracy. With a programme to win the support of the poorer sections of the peasantry and other exploited layers, such as the urban middle class and intelligentsia, landlordism and capitalism could be overthrown.

Through the victory of the international revolution in the more industrialised capitalist countries the building of socialism could begin. Triumphant revolution in these countries would end the isolation of other workers' states and because of their higher productivity level lay the basis for the construction of socialism - that is, a society of plenty where need is met. In this way the tasks of the bourgeois democratic revolution would be achieved by the working class as part of the international socialist revolution.

These were the classical ideas of the 'Permanent Revolution' that were developed from the experience of the Russian revolutions of 1905 and 1917. In particular they were developed by Trotsky and encompassed by Lenin.

In a distorted caricature of this Marxist prognosis the Cuban revolution would eventually result in the overthrow of landlordism and capitalism and replace it with a centrally planned economy. The revolution was to acquire mass support and bring tremendous benefits to the Cuban population. But the new regime which triumphed in 1959 would not be based upon a regime of workers' democracy.

Castro and the July 26th Movement

At the time of the Moncada attack Castro still pronounced his allegiance to the Ortodoxos. The party leadership regarded the attempted assault on the Moncada as an adventure. Large sections of the Ortodoxos and the urban middle class were still hoping to reach an agreement with the dictatorship. Batista denounced it as an attempted "communist putsch [coup]". The Communist Party denounced it as an attempt at a "bourgeois putsch".

US imperialism at the time was increasingly expressing its concern about what it viewed as "communist encroachment" throughout Latin America. Under pressure from Washington, after a visit to Havana by CIA director Allen Dulles, Batista agreed to the establishment of the Buró de Represión a las Actividades Comunistas BRAC.

Neither the CIA nor Batista had Castro and his supporters in mind when this special police unit was established. Reflecting how little his movement was perceived as a serious threat at the time, Castro and the other imprisoned insurgents were released in 1955 as a 'goodwill gesture' after a campaign to free them which in part was initiated by the Roman Catholic Church.

In Cuba Castro was heralded as a cause celebre because of his struggle against Batista and especially as a consequence of his imprisonment on the infamous Isle of Pines. The one condition of his release was that he should leave Cuba. He headed for Mexico where Cuban exiles and some of his followers had been congregating during the early 1950s.

Castro had established a reputation as an audacious and charismatic leader. As a 'Young Turk' in the movement he was able to exploit this to his maximum advantage. In the summer of 1955 his new group, the Movement of the 26th of July, was formally established and he broke from the Ortodoxos in 1956. At its launch the Movement declared that in its view the *"Jefferson philosophy was still valid"*. Thomas Jefferson was one of the eighteenth century leaders of the US war of independence against colonial British rule. His 'philosophy' was therefore liberal capitalism and parliamentary democracy. Castro viewed the USA as his model for Cuba.

Within the Ortodoxos movement a layer of its supporters were seeking negotiations and a compromise with the dictatorship. Others, especially the youth, were seeking more direct means of confronting the regime.

The prospects for Castro had been enhanced by the suicide of the former leader of the party, Eduardo Chibas, in 1951. By projecting himself in the image of a new Martí, Castro made an appeal to the ranks of the Ortodoxos to support him.

The Communist Party in Retirement

At the same time the expanding political vacuum was inflated by the situation in which the Cuban Communist Party (Partido Socialista Popular - PSP) found itself. Hugh Thomas in his book on Cuba accurately states: *" The Cuban Communists in general were in semi-retirement during most of these years, recovering their health and energies..."*

The party had lost much of its credibility as a consequence of its earlier policy of supporting a popular or people's front. The policy had been adopted by the Latin American communist parties after 1935 when a meeting of all the regional communist parties was called in Moscow where the new line was imposed in each country, with some exceptions such as Brazil.

It was adopted in Cuba during an exceptional period of social turmoil. 1933 had seen a radical revolt by junior officers in the army. Amongst other measures they demanded the ending of the Platt Amendment, signed with the USA in 1901, which gave the US the right to militarily intervene in Cuba. At the head of this movement was a young officer from a working class background, Batista.

This was a period of social upheaval and radicalisation in Cuba. There was a crisis of authority in the government. The one force which seemed able to hold things together was the army headed by the radicalised junior officers. Batista reflected the conflicts between the various classes which existed at the time. He reflected the pressure from a wing of the national ruling class to assert its own interests against US imperialism. At the same time he reflected the pressures from the working class and sections of the radicalised middle class for greater social change. For a period Batista balanced between the different class pressures which were bursting forth.

Batista ruled Cuba through a series of puppet presidents, granting concessions to workers and also implementing some land reform. A minimum wage was introduced and it was made illegal to dismiss employees 'without reason'. These measures were slow in being implemented but they boosted the confidence of the working class. Being a populist leader from a working class background allowed Batista to enjoy widespread support from the Cuban population for a short time. But like all bonapartist leaders and regimes - those which balance between various class interests combining reforms to the masses with repression - in the final analysis they act to defend one class or another, in this case the interests of capitalism. Batista proved to be no different.

Political opponents were viciously dealt with under Batista's regime. With the encouragement of the US ambassador, the army was deployed in 1935 against a general strike demanding a new democratic constitution. Despite his earlier populist nationalism, Batista succumbed to the pressures of imperialism and ultimately fully collaborated with it.

After winning the presidential elections in 1940 and withdrawing his candidature in 1944, Batista returned to power in a coup which was staged in 1952 after he lost another presidential election. The new hated regime which seized power in 1952 was to unleash repression and terror. The communists throughout this period adopted a policy of supporting Batista, slavishly following the decisions of the Moscow conference in 1935.

At its congress in 1939 the PSP agreed it should *"adopt a more positive attitude towards Colonel Batista"*. From that moment on in party journals Batista was no longer *"... the focal point of reaction; but the focal point of democracy"*. (New York *Daily Worker*, 1 October 1939)

The international organisation of the communist parties which existed at the time, the Comintern, stated in its journal: *"Batista... no longer represents the centre of reaction... the people who are working for the overthrow of Batista are no longer acting in the interests of the Cuban people."* (*World News and Views*, No 60, 1938).

In 1952 the PSP declared the new regime to be *"no different"* to the preceding one! The 'communists' had been loyal supporters of the Bonapartist dictator for more than a decade when he seized power. As Hugh Thomas comments in his book, the Catholic laity had endured more conflicts with the regime than the Communist Party leaders.

Despite this the PSP maintained an important influence amongst important sections of workers. Yet, in the course of events, the party paid a price for its collaboration with a loss of support amongst the working class and the youth.

However, the highest price was paid by the Cuban masses, suffering under a regime which rapidly showed itself to be puppet of US imperialism. Historically Cuba had been a playground for the 'gringos' north of the Rio Grande. Havana developed as the local brothel and gambling casino of US bankers and industrialists. Batista was merely the local pimp.

It was against this historical background that Che Guevara eventually found his way into the ranks of the July 26th Movement. Castro and his followers would undoubtedly have seemed a more attractive and combative force than the communist parties at the time. Che was in contact with some of Castro's supporters prior to his arrival in Mexico. Plans were already being laid to begin an armed struggle against Batista.

During 1954 Che was also mixing with Communist Party members from all over Latin America, especially exiles from Guatemala. Initially he saw his future within the Communist Party and wrote to his mother anticipating that he would eventually take such a path. But he held back at this time largely because the bohemian dragon within him had still not been fully slain. As Che himself admitted, he had *"well-defined convictions"* but also what he described as his *"vagabonding"* and *"repeated informality"*. As he explained in the letter to his mother he still yearned to travel especially through Europe and, *"I couldn't do that submitted to an iron discipline"*.

It was not until 1955 that he met Castro. The immediate prospect of a struggle which was offered to him by Castro and his movement together with his *"well-defined convictions"* finally led Che to accept that *"iron discipline"* which he had previously rejected, although it was not within the ranks of the Communist Party.

A Revolutionary Spirit

Che's entry into the July 26th Movement was not without its problems. Some of its members were of a pronounced middle class background and his political persona irritated them. Che, despite his lack of formal commitment to the movement, was showing aspects of his character which would emerge in a very forceful way during the rest of his revolutionary life.

He was austere and once he had decided to commit himself to revolutionary struggle, utterly self-sacrificing. Some of those who met him were somewhat 'put out' by what they regarded as Che's 'self-righteousness'. As Jon Anderson recounts in his biography, a Moncada veteran, Melba Hernández, had arrived in Mexico to join her husband. She was still dressed in refined clothes and jewellery when she was introduced to Che. He looked at her and proclaimed that she could not be a serious revolutionary dressed so: *"Real revolutionaries adorn themselves on the inside, not on the surface"* he stated.

Having joined the July 26th Movement, Che threw himself into it body and soul as preparations were undertaken to land in Cuba and begin the 'revolution' during 1956. He intensified his political studies and undertook an increasingly harsh physical training course putting himself on a diet to get fit. Still plagued by asthma he needed to be twice as healthy as other fighters. Through will-power and determination Che overcame the limitations his disability imposed upon him. Within the group, which numbered no more than twenty to thirty according to Castro, Che rapidly rose to pre-eminence.

The group was arrested in Mexico and then released. From prison Che wrote to his parents: *"My future is linked with that of the Cuban revolution. I either triumph with it or die there... From now on I wouldn't consider my death a frustration, only,*

Castro in May 1955, leaving the Cuban prison in which he had spent two years after the Moncada attack

like Hikmet [the Turkish poet]: I will take to the grave only the sorrow of an unfinished song".

His commitment to the cause of revolution was now his entire life. This spirit is indispensable to defeat capitalism and win a revolution. It is the quality in Che which those fighting to emancipate the working class and exploited classes today need to emulate.

As he engaged directly in revolutionary struggle his boldness and self-sacrifice was to become very evident. At the same time his ideas developed in a one-sided manner. He based himself on the peasantry and guerrilla struggle. This is one important aspect of the Marxist policy which applies in the rural areas where a peasant class exists.

The question of the role of the working class and the urban centres is also of decisive importance is the application of a correct Marxist policy. As will be further explained in this book this is true even in countries where the working class forms a relatively small section of the population.

Unfortunately because of the uneven development of Che's ideas it was not possible for him to develop a policy and programme which could bring about a victorious revolution in countries such as Argentina, Brazil or Chile where powerful working classes existed.

Guerrillaism & Marxism

NO REVOLUTIONARY develops ideas in a social vacuum or in total isolation. In this respect the ideas which Che Guevara developed and supported were not an exception. In looking at Che's life nobody who regards themself as a revolutionary, fighting against exploitation and oppression, can question his heroism, determination and self-sacrifice. By the time he arrived in Cuba he was wedded to the idea that socialism had to be built throughout Latin America to liberate the masses from exploitation and free the continent of imperialist domination.

However, what Che did not have was a clear understanding of how this could be done and which class would have to play the leading role in achieving it. From a Marxist point of view the most important deficiency in Che's ideas was his underestimation of the role of the working class in overthrowing capitalism and building socialism.

Because of the specific conditions which existed in Cuba this deficiency did not prevent the defeat of Batista or the coming to power of the guerrilla force Che was fighting with. Because of international factors and the momentum of the revolution, neither did it prevent the overthrow of capitalism in Cuba (discussed in later chapters).

Nonetheless, it did shape the character of the new regime which was to emerge after the triumph of the revolution. Moreover, when Che's ideas were later applied to other countries in Latin America, where objective conditions were very different, they failed. Many heroic and genuine revolutionaries used their energies and not a few gave their lives in trying to apply his incomplete ideas.

What Che had not absorbed from his studies of Marxist literature was the experience of the Russian revolution of 1917 and the ideas of the permanent revolution. In particular, he did not grasp the role of the working class even in countries where it constitutes a minority in society.

Unfortunately after the victory of the Russian working class the revolution was not victorious in the developed industrialised countries. The Bolshevik victory remained isolated. A combination of intervention by the armies of Western imperialism and civil war exhausted the Russian workers' movement. Whilst capitalism remained defeated in Russia for a prolonged historical period of time, until the capitalist restoration of 1989-92, the working class was robbed politically of its control of society. This was usurped through the emergence of a vicious, privileged bureaucratic elite.

Che failed to grasp the lessons of the revolution of 1917 or later events. To do this and apply the lessons of these events to the specific conditions which emerged in Central and Latin America required a gigantic and audacious leap forward in political understanding and vision. In isolation and under the influence of events and alternative ideas, Che could not complete the leap (which was and still is) required in applying the methods of Marxism to the particular conditions which exist on his continent.

Under capitalism the working class is compelled to struggle collectively through strikes, demonstrations and workplace occupations etc in order to win concessions and to defend its interests. Of course where necessary the workers' movement needs also to organise its own defence from armed attack by the employers and those who defend their interests.

The decisive role of the working class in the socialist revolution arises because of the collective class consciousness which it develops in the workplace and which allows it to prepare the basis for the collective democratic control and management of society. This lays the basis for establishing a workers' democracy in order to begin the task of building socialism. By incorporating into its socialist programme the interests of other exploited layers of society, the working class can win its support to carry through the revolution and overthrow landlordism and capitalism. In this way the proletariat plays the leading role in the revolution and the building of socialism.

The Rural Struggle and Marxism

The poorer peasants, whilst able to play an important revolutionary role in struggle, lack the collective class consciousness which predominates amongst the working class. The peasantry, because of its isolation in rural areas and economic relationship to the land, with its narrow, parochial and individualistic outlook, cannot play the same role in the revolution as the workers in the cities.

Whilst Marxism defends the leading role of the working class in the socialist revolution it also recognises the importance of the struggle in the countryside, especially amongst rural agricultural workers and the poorer sections of the peasantry.

Even today, after a massive urbanisation of society in South America, there are many important links between the rural areas and the urban population, especially the working class. This is pointedly the case in Central America. Workers from the cities will periodically return to the countryside for work or to support their families who are still there. Sections of the urban poor living in shanty-towns on the periphery of major cities live almost as peasants on the outskirts of the industrial centres.

These sections of the population are bound to be affected by the rural movements and will frequently take up the methods of struggle mainly used by peasants and rural workers. These methods of struggle will include land occupations and forming contingents of armed groups to fight the military, police and armed thugs used by the landlords to protect their interests. Under certain conditions these movements in the countryside can erupt prior to movements in the cities and can bring with them a boost in the confidence of urban workers.

This process has been seen in the Zapatista uprising in Mexico (a radical, rural guerrilla organisation) and by the explosive movement of the Brazilian landless organised in the MST (Movimiento Sem Terra).

A revolutionary Marxist programme would support such struggles in the countryside and take every step to incorporate them with the workers' movement in the cities. They would, however, play an auxiliary role to the movement in the cities.

Che, influenced by a combination of factors, drew other conclusions which underestimated the role of the working class. His conclusions evolved over a period of time. They were being formed through his observations, discussions and then his participation in the Cuban movement. His ideas were most clearly expressed in articles and publications after the conquest of power by the 26th July Movement in 1959. One of the most complete explanations of his policies is to be found in his book, *Guerrilla Warfare*, which was not published until 1960.

A Different Conception

Partly as a result of his own class background and the fact that he was not an active member of any organisation in the workers' movement, Che never actively participated in the actual struggles of the proletariat. Apart from some activity in Guatemala his only active participation in the revolutionary left was through the July 26th Movement and the guerrilla struggle in Cuba. As a result he failed to grasp the revolutionary potential and strength which workers possess as a class.

Other political ideas and experiences which he was exposed to inevitably had an important impact on the formulation of his hypothesis. He was bound to be under the influence of the powerful traditions of historical struggles throughout the Latin American continent. The wars for independence led by Simon Bolívar, who posed the idea of unifying the entire continent, Augusto Sandino's struggle in Nicaragua, Martí's in Cuba and others during the 19th century, together with the Mexican revolution (1910-18) and the peasant armies of Emiliano Zapata and Pancho Villa, all form part of a strong tradition on the continent which are engraved into the outlook of political activists.

These struggles took place in a previous historical epoch when the proletariat and the workers' movement were only in their very early stages of development. Since that period the working class has enormously developed throughout the region.

In Cuba by 1953, according to Hugh Thomas, only 42% of the working population was employed on the land. By the end of the 1950s there were about 200,000 peasant families and 600,000 rural workers. In the cities were to be found 400,000 families of the urban proletariat and 200,000 families of those employed as waiters, servants and street vendors. The social weight of the Cuban working class was far greater at the end of the 1950s than the Russian working class in 1917.

As well as the weight of historical tradition Che was also influenced at an early stage by the ideas expressed by the Peruvian, Pesce. Pesce articulated the theories which he and Mariátegui had begun to advocate during the 1920s. They revised the classical analysis of Marxism regarding the role of the working class and the peasantry, giving far more importance to the latter in the socialist revolution. Che was also attracted by the victory of Mao Zedong's peasant army in China in 1949, together with the ongoing national liberation struggle in Vietnam. Undoubtedly he was influenced by some of Mao's writings.

The Latin American communist parties, although formally adhering to the working class in the cities, followed the polices of supporting people's or popular fronts. This policy attempted to limit the struggles of the masses from going beyond the interests of capitalism. Che, along with a broader layer of youth in Latin America, regarded this policy as too 'dogmatic' and looked for something more 'radical'.

As far as Che was concerned the ideas he defended were an attempt to apply a fresh 'Marxist' approach to the specific conditions of Latin America. He was unable to formulate another alternative to the pusillanimous role of the communist parties apart from defending the guerrilla struggle as the driving force of the revolution throughout the continent.

As a result the leading class in the revolution was the "peasantry with a proletarian ideology", as he put it in a speech which was published in June 1960 entitled, *'The Responsibilities of the Working Class in Our Revolution'*, *"... It is no secret that the strength of the revolutionary movement was primarily among the peasants, and secondarily among the working class... Cuba, like all underdeveloped countries, does not have a powerful proletariat."* Che continued that *"... the worker at times became a privileged individual"*.

In reality the 'primary' position of the peasants in the revolution reduced the working class to an auxiliary role - the exact opposite of what Marxism explains is

Guerrilla struggle - The September 1958 Offensive

the class able to play the leading role in the revolution and in building socialism.

It was true that the workers in the cities in Cuba at the time did enjoy a higher standard of living than the peasants in the countryside. Behind the idea of a 'privileged' working class lay the idea that the revolutionary potential of any social grouping is only determined by the depth of its poverty. What Che missed was the potential role of the working class because of its position as a class. A contributory factor in Che reaching these conclusions was the timid role of the communist leaders.

In his book, *Guerrilla Warfare*, Che again plays down the potential role that the working class can play. Referring to the *"three contributions"* Cuba has made in revolutionary strategy Che argues: *"The third contribution is fundamentally of a strategic nature, and is a rebuke to those who dogmatically assert that the struggle of the masses is centred in the urban movements, totally forgetting the immense participation of the people from the countryside in the life of all the underdeveloped countries of Latin America."* He argued that the repressive conditions which exist in the cities made it more difficult for the organised workers' movement. The situation, he said, was easier in the countryside where the inhabitants could be *"supported by armed guerrillas"*.

Che again missed the central point about the role of the workers as a class in building socialism and reduced the question of revolution to one important issue, logistics. The issue is how the difficulties which the movement in the cities encounters can be overcome. Che, unfortunately fled from this issue to the mountains where the guerrillas can 'support' the local inhabitants.

Foco Theory

In the same book he argued that *"... the arena for the armed struggle must basically be the countryside"*. The guerrilla centres would rest upon the support of the peasantry and would act to ignite a movement to overthrow the established regimes - the 'foco' theory. While Che advocated this thesis it was developed further by Regis Debra, the French intellectual who generalised it for the continent and beyond. Che echoed Debra in 1963 in an article entitled, *'Building a Party of the Working Class'*: *"We went from the countryside to the city, from lesser to greater, creating the revolutionary movement that culminated in Havana"*.

Rather than the guerrillas "creating" the revolutionary movement, they were able to step into a political vacuum and seize the initiative. This was possible because of the specific objective situation which unfolded in Cuba. When Che attempted to apply his ideas to other countries in Latin America they were a failure.

Marxists recognise that under certain specific conditions a guerrilla struggle in the countryside where the working class is not playing the leading role may be victorious in overthrowing an existing regime.

However, without the working class consciously at the head of the revolutionary process, it will not be possible to establish a new regime based upon workers' democracy which could begin the task of constructing socialism.

Despite Che's wrong approach to these questions, his support for the idea of socialism was to have a profound effect on developments inside the July 26th Movement and on the future direction of the revolutionary processes in Cuba.

Granma & the July 26th Movement

On 2 DECEMBER 1956 eighty two men landed on the Cuban coast having sailed from Mexico in a run down boat, *Granma*. The voyage and landing were little short of a disaster. A journey which was planned to last five days had taken seven. At times the trip was almost comical. As they approached the Cuban coastline the navigator fell overboard.

The landing was supposed to have coincided with an armed uprising in the city of Santiago following which 100 insurgents should have awaited the arrival of *Granma* with trucks and supplies. Frank País, a leader of the July 26th Movement in the Oriente province, was to organise this. He was later on to organise supplies for the rebel army through the underground urban network which was built, the Llano.

After the *Granma* weighed anchor the plan was then to launch an attack on the towns of Niquero and Manzanillo before proceeding to the Sierra Maestra mountain range from where Castro intended to launch the war against Batista in earnest.

Batista had dispatched extra troops to Oriente province and crushed the uprising in Santiago while naval and air force patrols awaited the arrival of Castro and his party. The insurgency began badly and got worse.

The rebels waded ashore in broad daylight, they were a mile short of their intended rendezvous, had left most of their supplies behind, and their reception party had given up and departed the night before after waiting for two days. On top of that they were spotted by an air force observation aircraft. The group was divided into two and roamed around lost for two days.

As Che described later in his diary they were *"disorientated and walking in circles, an army of shadows, of phantoms walking as if moved by some obscure psychic mechanism"*. They finally regrouped and headed eastwards towards the Sierra mountains under the guidance of a local peasant. They encountered the first attack from the Cuban army during which Che suffered a superficial wound in the neck.

Gruelling war

This was the opening phase of a gruelling war which was to last for two years. It ended in January 1959 after Batista had fled the country on New Year's Eve. The forces of the 26th of July Movement marched into Havana to be greeted by a general strike of the workers. Of the eighty two who came ashore from Granma just over twenty eventually regrouped in the Sierra Maestro. Less would see the New Year in 1959 and the triumph of the revolution.

How was it possible for such a small group to emerge triumphant within two short, if bloody and turbulent, years? The answer lies in a combination of political and social factors. Firstly, social support for Batista was disintegrating. Opposition to the dictatorship was increasing and the regime by 1959 was on the point of collapse. Even the army was beginning to be affected and became increasingly demoralised.

At the same time none of the opposition parties channelled the anger of the population. The docile PSP was largely compromised by its previous support for Batista. The party still had a certain authority amongst important sections of industrial workers in the cities. However, its leaders largely used the authority they had to keep the workers' movement in check.

As the result of this, a political vacuum had developed in Cuba. Castro and his forces, despite being relatively small, were able to fill it after a two year struggle which they conducted from the Sierra Maestro. By the end of 1958 Castro had no more than 3,000 in his army and this included a large number of non-combatants who were based in camps.

If the war which was fought between 1956-58 is considered from merely a military point of view then Castro won a remarkable victory. The Prussian general and writer, Karl Clausewitz, argued: *"War is not merely a political act, but also a real political instrument, a continuation of political commerce, a carrying out of the same by other means."* It was the objective political situation and social factors which had unfolded in Cuba that permitted Castro to score such a dramatic victory in only two years.

To achieve this victory, subjective questions, in particular the collapse of the morale of the Cuban army and the will power and determination of the fighters of the July 26th Movement played a crucial part.

Due to the hatred of Batista by the mass of the Cuban population the guerrillas could rely upon the support they enjoyed amongst the peasants and urban population. There was no other political force which was seen as waging an effective or serious struggle against the regime.

This support increased as the war raged and the brutality of the regime was increasingly contrasted with the heroism of Castro's fighters. Moreover in battle, when Batista's soldiers were taken prisoners, unlike captured guerrilla fighters, they were not executed. They were discussed with and then set free unharmed. Such initiatives had a big effect in undermining the morale of the soldiers in Batista's army. Castro lost no opportunity in trying to present himself as a modern José Martí

- a new liberator of Cuba.

Che Guevara emerged as one of the principal military and political leaders. He had originally enlisted as the medical expert. Events forced him in another direction as he displayed other outstanding qualities in the thick of war. Early on in the conflict he crossed yet another line in the evolution of his own character. Caught in an exchange between guerrillas and the army, in a split second, he was forced to choose between picking up medical supplies or a machine gun and ammunition.

Opting for the latter it became clear that despite his medical knowledge and experience Che was not destined to play the role of doctor.

As the war progressed Che's authority increased in the eyes of his fellow rebels. He actively engaged in battles with the army and undertook quite reckless missions on occasions. During one air raid, as other rebels fled including Castro, Che remained behind to help stranded fighters. He was eventually appointed commander of his own column along with Castro's brother, Raúl.

Che's overall maxim was to lead by example, never to ask those under his command to do what he would not undertake himself. He also refused all privileges - few though they were for those fighting in the Sierra Maestra. Che's own conditions were in many ways worse than the soldiers he fought with. The effects of his crippling asthma attacks in the jungle would have driven many with less determination away from the battleground.

Suicide Squad

The column of fighters he led were undoubtedly amongst the most determined and heroic. They were fuelled by his bold example and determination to achieve a victorious revolution.

They were steeled to continue the struggle against what at times seemed impossible odds. The 'Suicide Squad', which was established in his column to undertake particularly dangerous missions, gained a fearsome reputation for its discipline and heroism.

It was a model for other rebel fighters to aspire to. Che noted in his wartime diaries: *"The 'Suicide Squad' was an example of revolutionary morale and only selected volunteers joined it. But whenever a man died - and it happened in every battle - when a new candidate was named, those not chosen would be grief-stricken and even cry. How curious to see those seasoned and noble warriors showing their youth by their tears of despair, because they did not have the honour of being in the front line of combat and death."*

There was another reason his column was amongst the most combative. Che began to organise a programme of political education for some of its members. His socialist ideas began to take root amongst many of his guerrillas as his reputation grew. In the midst of the military conflict there was also a political dispute which unfolded within the July 26th Movement. It featured a power struggle between the guerrilla movement in the mountains and the urban underground resistance, the Llano. At the same time it also posed the question of what the July 26th Movement stood for. Che's outspoken defence of socialist ideas was a minority voice within the ensuing polemics.

Character of July 26th Movement

The July 26th Movement's ideology and programme reflected the social composition of much of its membership and supporters. The bulk of the leaders were drawn from the urban middle class, some from its upper layers. Whilst the Movement did have a layer of lower middle class and even working class members, as was reflected by the social make-up of those who participated in the Moncada incident, it was not a political current which was given birth to by the working class.

Castro had established an inner core of leaders based upon the steering committee which he had set up in the summer of 1955. This reflected much of the Movement at that time. Most were former students from the urban upper middle class. The National Directorate (of which Castro was not a member) was made up of such people and was responsible for all the underground activity in the urban areas, ie obtaining the supplies of arms and communications, etc. Many were self-sacrificing and had been arrested and tortured by Batista's police. However, politically what united them was the struggle to overthrow Batista and little else.

The programme and ideology of the July 26th Movement reflected the vacillations and amorphous features which are the political hallmarks of the urban petty bourgeoisie. Most of its members probably wanted little more than to establish a capitalist parliamentary democracy and enact a radical democratic programme of reform.

Che had many presentiments about Castro's colleagues from the urban centres in the National Directorate: *"Through isolated conversations, I discovered the evident anti-Communist inclinations of most of them,"* he wrote in his diary.

There was a more radical wing to the movement which in many ways Castro represented. He wrote an *'Appeal to the Cuban People',* which was very combative. In defence of the guerrillas' proclamation to burn sugar cane he wrote: *"To those who invoke the workers' livelihoods to combat this measure, we ask: Why don't they defend the workers when... they suck dry their salaries, when they swindle their retirement pensions, when they pay them in bonds and they kill them from hunger during eight months? Why are we spilling our blood if not for the poor of Cuba? What does a little hunger today matter if we can win the bread and liberty of tomorrow?"*

Although from a Marxist point of view the idea of small groups of guerrillas burning sugar cane and imposing a struggle on behalf of the sugar cane workers, rather than drawing them into struggle, is wrong, the radical sentiments behind such declarations received an echo from Cuba's poor.

However, the programme which even Castro was advocating in the early stages of the war, albeit with a social conscience, did not go beyond the bounds of capitalism. During the first few months of 1957 a leading correspondent of the New York Times, Herbert Matthews, who had also reported on the Spanish civil war, secured a visit and interview with Castro.

When published in February it landed as an international bomb shell and was a publicity coup for Castro as Batista was claiming the guerrilla leader had been killed in battle. Apart from being a major international propaganda success for Castro, the interview revealed much about his political ideas at the time.

Matthews wrote: *"It is a revolutionary movement that calls itself socialistic. It is also nationalistic, which generally means anti-Yankee. The programme is vague and couched in generalities, but it amounts to a new deal for Cuba, radical, democratic and therefore anti-Communist. The real core of its strength is that it is fighting against the military dictatorship of President Batista...[Castro] has strong ideas of liberty, democracy, social justice, the need to restore the Constitution, to hold elections."*

Castro told Matthews: *"You can be sure that we have no animosity towards the United States and the American people... we are fighting for a democratic Cuba and an end to the dictatorship. We are not anti-military... for we know the men are good and so are many of the officers."*

During the interview Castro succeeded in giving Matthews the impression that he had more forces around him than was the case. In conditions of war this was legitimate - why show the enemy Batista one's weaknesses. Matthews reported that eighty two of the original Granma landing were with Castro and that his forces were growing all the time as more and more youth arrived.

In fact, as Hugh Thomas recounts, Castro's brother kept passing in front of Matthews with the same group of men dressed differently. Castro had no more than eighteen in camp with him at the time and a total armed force of twenty!

It is probably accurate to conclude that Castro at that time did not have a worked out political philosophy. According to one account even by 1960 Castro was still not supporting 'socialism'. Che, in conversation with a friend from Mexico, Dr David Mitrani, stated that he hoped to transform Cuba into a socialist state but that Fidel was not yet convinced (See Jon Anderson's biography).

Since the victory of the Cuban revolution it has been argued that the overthrow of capitalism was anticipated by Castro and even prepared in collaboration with the bureaucracy which then ruled in Moscow. This analysis overestimates the political clarity with which the leaders of the July 26th Movement approached the situation

"Happy 1958" - celebrating the first year in the mountains

in Cuba. It also falsely elevates the role of the bureaucracy in Moscow in overthrowing landlordism and capitalism in Cuba.

The process of the revolution, together with a combination of national and international factors, propelled the central players in these events to a political and social location which was not their intended point of arrival. Che stated in 1960: *"The principal actors of this revolution had no coherent viewpoint."* (*Notes for the Study of the Ideology of the Cuban Revolution*)

The impact of big social events, especially wars and the struggle between different classes in society, has affected the political outlook of many individuals. Che Guevara had empirically arrived at the guerrilla war in which he was now engaged against the Batista dictatorship. The effects of the guerrilla war had an important effect in radicalising its primary leaders. Che wrote to Ernesto Sábato, a prominent Argentinean novelist, in a letter in April 1960: *"The war revolutionised us... In this way our revolution was born. In this way, its slogans were being created, and in this way little by little, we began drawing theoretical conclusions in the heat of these events to create our own body of ideas."*

Che was the most politically sophisticated of the leading guerrilla fighters in the sense of advocating an alternative ideology. From the standpoint of a Marxist analysis the theoretical conclusions he eventually drew were false and in many respects quite crude. However, he asserted a growing influence over Castro as events and the struggle unfolded. Both were propelled by the rhythm of events and the concrete situation in which they found themselves.

Whilst Che aspired to conquering a socialist revolution with an internationalist character he had no worked out perspective or programme of how to achieve his aim. By his own admission the ideas he developed evolved empirically, shaped more by his own subjective experiences than by an extensive appreciation of the historical lessons of the international workers' movement.

A Difference of Opinion

Within the July 26th Movement things did not remain politically static during the course of the civil war. A conflict emerged between the National Directorate and the guerrilla leadership in the Sierra. Castro wanted to establish his rebel army as the primary leadership in the movement - under his control.

Initially this friction was kept within manageable limits. It surfaced at a meeting in 1957 where some of the urban leaders argued for Castro to leave the Sierra Maestra to raise funds on a speaking tour. Along with other proposals this clearly indicated they wanted to play down the importance of the guerrilla struggle in the Sierra Maestra. On this occasion Castro won the day and gained a majority against other proposals.

Over the following months this friction was to develop into an open political rift between the Llano and the guerrilla leaders. The latter in the main thought the leadership of the Llano was pusillanimous - and not without justification. On the National Directorate were some of the most conservative sections of the July 26th Movement.

However, a contributing element in the friction was another political factor. Those involved in fighting a guerrilla war, however self-sacrificing, develop a certain contempt towards the urban population. The desperate hardship involved in the struggle in the mountains can wrongly lead the rural fighters to dismiss the masses in the cities as unwilling to struggle because of their relatively privileged situation. This attitude is reinforced if the guerrilla fighters lack clear political ideas and are not linked to an organised movement of urban workers with an audacious leadership and socialist policies.

Castro certainly still lacked a clear political objective for his struggle beyond overthrowing the dictatorship. What he did have was an ability to rest opportunistically on numerous political forces to strengthen his own position. On 12 July 1957 Castro signed a pact with the openly pro-capitalist Auténtico and Ortodoxo parties which had rejected Batista's recent attempt to buttress his regime by calling presidential elections in which he himself would not stand.

The deal known as the 'Sierra Pact' limited the July 26th Movement in its objectives. Whilst it called for Batista's resignation and rejected the military junta, it proposed an 'independent' member from civic institutions to act as transitional president and for full elections within twelve months. Its economic programme was limited to little more than agrarian reform. If anything it was even more moderate than the original programme of the July 26th Movement and intended to contain the political situation in the interests of capitalism and imperialism should Batista fall.

However, reflected in the signing of this agreement was the fact that the Batista regime was increasingly losing the support it enjoyed and opposition to it was growing. Castro's guerrilla fighters had begun to attract a layer of youth from the urban centres. Some protests were taking place in the cities. There was a certain shift in the policy of the PSP. Though still regarding Castro's military campaign as an adventure some contact began to take place between the guerrillas and the PSP.

The PSP used these contacts to try and persuade Castro that conditions were not right for an armed movement in Cuba and to urge him to wait for a more opportune moment. Consequently relations between the PSP and Castro were strained but contact was maintained.

The eighth Congress of the PSP was held in 1957 at which the leadership announced that the PSP recognised the *"valour and sincerity"* of Castro. At the same time the party also made clear that it had a *"radical disagreement with the tactics and plans"* of Castro. The party concluded that the July 26th Movement had not yet taken a sufficiently anti-imperialist line. In PSP jargon that meant that it was not sufficiently anti-USA and pro-Russian. The party called for elections and the formation of a *"popular front"* involving the *"national bourgeoisie"*.

This position was not without opposition from within the party especially its youth wing. Whilst the PSP played no real role in the movement which was unfolding, apart from trying to act as a restraining influence on Castro, during 1958 an increasing number of young party members joined the rebels in the mountains - especially the columns under the leadership of Che and Raúl Castro.

Enter US Imperialism

US imperialism was evidently beginning to become increasingly worried about the situation. In general the main concern it had was to safeguard its business interests and contain unrest. Violence was not good for a return on investment. Batista was encouraged to 'democratise' and hold elections which would be won by a 'safe' traditional party. The emergence of Castro's forces and their continued campaign had complicated the situation.

Between 1957 and 1958 there was a division of opinion in Washington about how to deal with the situation. The State Department, CIA and Department of Defence had their own separate policies. They were not always compatible. The Department of Defence and US military in Cuba, working together with and arming BRAC (the anti-communist bureau), wanted to support Batista and crush the guerrilla movement.

At the same time the State Department, apparently in agreement with the CIA, wanted Batista out as the most effective manner of controlling the situation. There is even evidence to suggest that they attempted to try and collaborate with and buy-off the July 26th Movement and Castro, in case he succeeded in overthrowing Batista.

According to Yuri Paporov, a KGB (Secret service of the USSR) official, CIA money was channelled to the July 26th Movement. This claim has been confirmed by Tad Szulc, Castro's biographer, who said it occurred between 1957 and 1958, after the 'Pact of Sierra Maestra' was signed by Castro!

This policy changed later as it became clear they could not control Castro or his movement.

Despite the apparent efforts by a section of the ruling class in the USA to reach out to Castro's movement, with a view to embracing its now internationally renowned leader, events conspired against this policy. The momentum of the revolutionary processes which was underway, together with questions of national prestige and individual interests, made this task initially difficult and ultimately unachievable.

Che's reputation was growing and he was increasingly known as an important 'communist' influence within the guerrilla forces. This increased the tension between the more pronounced 'anti-Communists' in the July 26th Movement, especially sections of its Llano leadership, and Che. He established his own line of supplies to his forces excluding the local leadership of the Llano in the Oriente province. This was headed by a member of the Directorate, Daniel. Che's actions undercut the authority of Daniel's leadership and provoked a clash. The Llano leadership appealed to Castro to arbitrate.

Behind this dispute was a broader political question which involved the increasing suspicion which existed between Che and the Llano leadership. Things came to a climax over a fresh political initiative. There was an attempt to form a coalition 'revolutionary' government in exile. It would be dominated by the July 26th Movement together with the Auténticos, led by Carlos Prío Socarrás. According to Armando Hart, the Llano leader involved in negotiations, the discussions had included some people *"close to the US embassy"*.

Miami Versus Sierra

The US, uncertain that Batista could hold on, attempted to patch together a coalition of anti-Batista forces within which they were hoping to included a 'controlled' July 26th Movement. A meeting was called in Miami which Castro ordered a delegation to attend. On 1 November the *'Cuban Liberation Junta'* was

Late 1958 - speaking to civilians in the town of Cabaiguán after a series of attacks on Army Garrisons

formed and the Miami Pact was signed.

Felipe Pazos had acted as the July 26th Movement's official leader in the delegation. He had done so without the consent of Castro who correctly saw it as a bid to upstage him. The pact which was agreed amounted to a clear attempt to secure the most moderate of regimes possible should Batista fall.

It included nothing opposing foreign intervention, said nothing against the idea of establishing a military junta to replace Batista and urged the incorporation of Castro's guerrilla forces into the Cuban army. In effect it was a proposal to prepare a tame post-Batista government and to dissolve the guerrilla forces.

When news of the agreement reached the Sierra Maestra it provoked outrage. Raúl Castro demanded that the July 26th Movement representatives be shot. Fidel Castro did not immediately respond. Che exploded with rage. He linked the acceptance of the Miami pact by the Directorate's representatives with his own conflicts with them over military issues. He accused them of *"sabotage"*.

Che had been involved in military action at the time. He was forced to retreat to a place called El Hombrito and was later injured at Altos de Conrado. Both of these setbacks were linked to the Directorate not sending him supplies. Now he issued an ultimatum in a letter sent to Castro on 9 December. Che demanded that he be allowed to take firm action against the Directorate or he would resign.

Castro's reply would determine not only his relations with Che but would affect the rest of the conduct of the guerrilla campaign. He was under pressure from those fighting in the mountains and was implicitly threatened by Pazos who was making a bid not only for the leadership of the July 26th Movement but also for the presidency in a post-Batista Cuba.

Castro moved firmly against the Directorate and the Miami pact: *"The leadership of the struggle against tyranny is, and will continue to be, in Cuba and in the hands of revolutionary fighters."* The National Directorate was accused of showing *"lukewarm patriotism and cowardice".* To try and head off Pazos's bid for a future presidency he made his own nomination - an elderly jurist Manuel Urruitia - to lead a transitional government.

The newly created junta collapsed, Pazos resigned from the Movement and the new leader of the Directorate, Faure Chomón, attacked Castro for his actions. Castro by his actions was making clear that he and his forces were the dominant alternative leadership to Batista. To consolidate his position he had to rest on Che and the 'left-wing' of the July 26th Movement in order to oppose the 'rightist' Directorate.

A total rupture with the Directorate was set to take place in the following months, propelled further by the process of events and the revolution. Che had played an important role in the outcome of this crossroads in the political evolution of Castro, the July 26th Movement and the revolution.

Che wrote to Daniel defending his 'Marxism', attacking the 'rightist Directorate' for allowing the movement's *"ass to be buggered"* by the Miami pact, and praising Castro as *"an authentic leader of the leftist bourgeoisie".* Even at this stage Che evidently did not see Castro as an ardent defender of socialism but as a representative of the radical bourgeoisie.

Daniel replied, expressing doubts about the Miami pact but urging the July 26th Movement to decide which path it intended taking and to ask itself where it was heading. This exchange echoed a furious ideological struggle which was taking place within the anti-Batista forces, including within the July 26th Movement.

As the crisis intensified the vacillating petty bourgeoisie who were grouped into this movement were being increasingly divided into opposing and separate camps.

On the one side the rightist leadership of the Directorate was increasingly under the influence of US imperialism and its attempts to achieve the most favourable outcome for itself.

Alternatively, a more combative wing was increasingly being radicalised to the left by a combination of the effects of the war, the process of the revolution and the necessity to defend its own interests and aspirations. Castro was now firmly entrenched as the leader of this wing - El Jefe Máximo as he became known.

Within this process Che was the most politically conscious in his support for international socialism. Although he lacked the clarity of ideas and programme which were needed to achieve this goal, the clash with the Directorate indicated he probably increasingly influenced Castro at critical moments and 'helped' him to take one or more steps further in a leftward direction.

By March 1958 the situation in Batista's camp was worsening. With difficulties mounting on all fronts the state apparatus was beginning to crack around him. In an unprecedented move a Havana magistrate agreed to prosecute a police colonel and the Chief of Naval Intelligence, Emilio Laurent, for the murder of four youths. All the schools were closed as 75,000 students went on strike. Batista suspended all civil rights and imposed radio and press censorship.

The General Strike - A Setback

There had been much speculation and discussion amongst the anti-Batista forces about the calling of a general strike. Despite having organised groups of supporters in the cities the organised basis of the July 26th Movement amongst the working class was weak. The main structured and coherent political force amongst the industrial workers was the PSP.

The Llano leadership refused to involve the PSP in its general strike plans. Formally the PSP supported the idea of a general strike although its leaders did nothing to prepare for one and worked against the July 26th Movement. The leadership of the official trade union federation, the CTC (Cuban Workers' Confederation) was corrupt and compromised through its relations with Batista. Despite being heavily influenced by the PSP it did not endorse or mobilise for the strike. The Llano leadership issued a call for a general strike on 9 April.

It was done with no preparation amongst the workers and without concrete plans or a strategy to conduct it. Even clandestine strike committees of activists and known fighters were not established in the workplaces to prepare the strike.

A general strike can arise, take form and play one of two roles for the workers' movement. If the social and political conditions are right it can directly challenge the ruling regime and dominant class in society. As a result it can pose the question of which class ought to run society - the capitalists and landlords or the working class with the support of other exploited social layers.

With a farsighted Marxist leadership such a conflict in society can develop into a revolutionary situation and victory for the proletariat. This situation usually arises when the ruling class is split and divided, the intermediary classes - the urban middle class and sections of the peasants - are politically vacillating and looking for an alternative, and the working class is prepared to fight to take over the running of society with a tested revolutionary leadership at its head.

In other situations, where the working class is newer, too weak or lacking experience, confidence and consciousness in itself as a class, a general strike can play a different role. Under these conditions, whilst the elements outlined above may exist, they are not sufficiently matured to actually allow the question of which class is to run society to be posed immediately. A strike under these conditions can play an important role in the working class gaining experience, building its organisations

Havana, New Years Day, 1959 - After hearing of Batista's flight, underground rebals take to the streets

and acquiring greater consciousness and confidence in itself as a class.

On 9 April 1958 neither situation arose. The all-out strike did not materialise and was a complete flop. In Havana the harbour functioned along with the transport system, and most shops and factories remained open. The strike was imposed over the heads of the workers and was ignored by them. The membership of the Havana strike committee illustrates the absence of participation from the workers. Apart from two members of the National Directorate of the July 26th Movement, it comprised of a senior engineer, a journalist from the Orthodox Party, the leader of the Cuban evangelical churches and a philanthropic doctor.

Castro had backed the strike but criticised the Llano leadership for excluding the PSP earlier. The PSP, with some justification, blamed the failure of 9 April on the July 26th Movement's "unilateral call" for a general strike.

The Batista regime's sense of security temporarily and falsely increased as a result of the strike's failure. Within the July 26th Movement it had deeper repercussions. The friction between the Llano and Sierra Maestra shot up as Castro turned the urban leadership's weakened prestige to his own advantage.

It was not revealed until years later the full significance of these events. Che wrote an article in 1964, entitled, 'A Decisive Meeting', for Verde Olivo, the magazine of the post-Batista army. Here the consequences of the events surrounding the April 'strike' become clear.

A meeting took place on 3 May 1958 in which an open struggle erupted between the supporters of the Llano and Castro. Arising from this meeting Castro was named for the first time general secretary of the July 26th Movement. This served to consol-

Early January 1959 - Castro's army enters Santa Clara in the final push to Havana

idate Castro's position as the leader of the movement. Che commented in his article: *"At this meeting decisions were taken that confirmed Fidel's moral authority, his indisputable stature... Fidel's standing and authority were consolidated, and he was named commander-in-chief of all forces, including the militias - which until then had been under Llano leadership..."*

Politically the defeat of the strike reinforced the scepticism in which the Sierra held the prospects of a movement in the cities. This was reflected in the struggle which took place in the meeting held on 3 May. The prominent role of the guerrilla struggle in the mountains was confirmed after the heated debate which took place. Che wrote: *"But most importantly, the meeting discussed and passed judgement on two conceptions that had clashed with each other throughout the whole previous stage of directing the war. The guerrilla conception would emerge triumphant from that meeting."*

He went on: *"We did away with various naive illusions about attempted revolutionary general strikes when the situation had not matured sufficiently to bring about such an explosion, and without having laid the necessary groundwork.... we had considered it likely that the Movement's forces would fail in attempting a revolutionary general strike..."*

Che qualifies his conclusions about the revolutionary general strike with references to central subjective and objective issues of *"groundwork"* and conditions which were not sufficiently *"matured"*. These are decisive questions but they are axiomatic for Marxists and centre on an estimation of the balance of forces which exist.

Che's consideration of the general strike as a *"naive illusion"* and counterpoising it with the *"guerrilla conception"* reveals how he and the leadership of the Sierra were not looking for the active and conscious participation of the masses, especially the proletariat, in the revolution. This was not simply a question of one article but an approach which was contained in his method.

If the *"groundwork"* for a general strike had not been prepared the job of Marxists was to prepare it. If the objective conditions are not *"sufficiently matured"* then Marxists patiently but energetically participate in the struggles of workers and conduct propaganda and agitation to assist them.

There was no assessment of the defeat of the general strike from a Marxist point of view by the leadership of the Llano. Its leaders did not subscribe to socialism, even less to revolutionary Marxism and its method of struggle aimed at ensuring the working class was running society.

The failure of the general strike in April reflected a certain paralysis by the working class in the cities, mainly because of the absence of a leadership able to offer a way forward. The July 26th Movement, whilst enjoying much sympathy because of its anti-Batista struggle, was not rooted amongst the proletariat and could not win its confidence due to its vague radical democratic programme.

The programme of the July 26th Movement in the Llano still reflected the aspirations of the radical petty bourgeoisie rather than those of the working class despite its call for action against the regime. However, this merely expanded the vacuum which existed in Cuban society. The failure of the general strike was not a measure of the support which Batista enjoyed. It was a measure of the absence of leadership within the workers' movement.

Castro's guerrilla army was perceived as being more combative and radical. Through its heroic military struggle and apparently uncompromising stand against the regime and US imperialism, it was increasingly able to fill the void which existed.

Batista, encouraged by the defeat of the April strike, mounted a military offensive against the rebels in May. His confidence evidently rose after the April events. However, this eventually collapsed given the poor state of morale within his forces. By July there was a definite change. Increasingly sections of Batista's army, including officers, came over to the side of the rebels.

In the final months of 1958 the rebels scored success after success on the battlefield. Other political and military opposition groups collapsed into Castro's forces. Che led his own column and spearheaded a major offensive on Cuba's fourth largest city, Santa Clara, which was Batista's main line of defence. The battle was crucial and lasted about three days during which Che played quite an heroic role, his forces at one stage seizing control of an armoured train. Che's rebels issued a call to arms as sections of the town's population took to the streets with Molotov cocktails and did battle with the army.

As the rebels strengthened their position, in the USA both the CIA and State Department had changed their earlier attitude and now regarded Castro's forces as too 'unreliable' to do business with. Almost giving up on the situation there was a lastditch attempt to put together a plan to replace Batista but it came to nothing due to a combination of treachery and the dynamic of the revolution which was underway.

With his regime in a state of disintegration, Batista fled the country on New Year's Day 1959 on board an air-force jet. On the night of 1/2 January Che arrived in Havana whilst Castro took control of Santiago. On 2 January, as Radio Rebelde reported the fall of Batista, the July 26th Movement issued a call for a general strike to mark the end of the old regime. On this occasion the strike was solid.

The rebels had won and they arrived in the capital to a rapturous reception as the population took to the streets. The hated Batista dictatorship had fallen. The revolution was set to continue. Its repercussions were to be felt around the globe.

In Power: Cuba versus 'the Gringos'

THE FALL of the Batista dictatorship did not end the revolutionary process which had developed in Cuba. Castro's triumphant entry into Havana represented the close of chapter one. A combination of factors came together and propelled the revolution much further than many of its leaders initially intended.

A provisional government was appointed which included Pazos, one of the Maestro pact signatories, and was under the presidency of Judge Manuel Urruita. All were under the umbrella of the July 26th Movement and Castro's guiding influence. It was precisely what its name stated - a movement and not a disciplined political party with a clear ideology or policy. The paralysis of 'liberal' capitalist Cuba was reflected in their acceptance of this 'provisional government'. The government rapidly announced that the elections would be postponed for eighteen months. The avowedly 'liberal' capitalist representatives lacked the vision or initiative to boldly enter the political fray. They had no choice but to allow Castro to pull the strings.

During the early days of January Castro played a typical bonapartist balancing act. On the one hand he incorporated sections of the 'liberal' Cuban capitalist class into the government and verbally tried to reassure them and to some extent US imperialism that their interests were not placed in jeopardy by the revolution against Batista. He was still motivated by the radical ideas of Martí more than anything else. The revolution he promised was genuinely *"Cuban, national and democratic"*. On 16 January he spoke at the grave of Eduardo Chibas (the former leader of the Orthodox Party), refuting that he was a communist and praising Chibas. Chibas had always been a bitter opponent of socialist ideas. At the end of January, when he was in Venezuela, Castro promised elections to a 'congress' within two years.

At the same time the workers, peasants, youth and even the middle class had been radicalised by the downfall of Batista. Castro rested on this mass movement as he moved to introduce measures which would assert Cuba's independence. He was also affected by it and pushed in an even more radical direction.

A combination of these processes at home and the reaction of US imperialism to these events resulted in the revolution going much further and faster forward than

Havana, may Day, 1963 - The "Big Three" of the Cuban Revolution - Che, Raúl and Fidel Castro

its central players had originally intended. US imperialism was horrified at events that began to unfold in its former playground.

The remaining US tourists staying at the Havana Hilton were undoubtedly somewhat disgruntled as this luxury hotel was transformed into an unofficial but defacto seat of government. As they abandoned holidays prematurely they were forced to mix with 'dirty' bearded armed guerrillas, workers and youth who now roamed the corridors. Amongst them was the figure who was increasingly becoming their bête noire - Che Guevara.

The Jury of a Million

During January measures began to be taken by Castro, largely under Che's direction, which aroused the wrath of US imperialism. In order to protect itself from the threat of a counter-revolution from the remnants of Batista's regime a purge of the old repressive state apparatus began to be implemented. Known sympathisers and supporters of Batista were arrested, known torturers and thugs were executed. Over a period of months several hundred were executed.

Che was a crucial influence in enacting these justifiable measures to safeguard the revolution. In mid-January Che established the Academia Militar-Cultural to conduct an education programme amongst the army at La Cabaña. From here two critical aspects of work were conducted. A political education programme amongst the army was launched. About 1,000 prisoners of war were held from Batista's defeated forces.

Che was trying through these measures to rebuild the army and by doing so construct it as a firm basis for the revolution. The guerrilla units and their leaders were incorporated into it increasingly with members of the PSP with whom Che was establishing closer relations.

From La Cabaña he oversaw the revolutionary tribunals which were used as a means of purging the army of its most pro-Batista elements. The trials centred on those who conducted torture and murder under the Batista dictatorship. Much of the Cuban population was in the mood to unleash lynching parties on those associated with the dictatorship. The tribunals provoked a massive attack by US imperialism which denounced such measures as criminal. However, the reprisals had the support of the mass of Cubans, especially the poor, who had suffered horrific crimes at the hands of Batista's thugs.

The tribunals were not elected committees of workers, soldiers and representatives of the local community as would have been advocated by Marxists during such revolutionary conditions.

However, the measures taken by the tribunals were to defend the revolution and to try and exact some justice for the victims of Batista's sadistic torturers. Those accused were given defence lawyers and the right to disprove or justify their actions. According to those who participated, in the main, nobody was shot for hitting a prisoner of the former regime. Only in the cases of brutal torture or death, which involved hundreds of cases, was execution the verdict. Former prisoners and the families of the dead or 'disappeared' were asked to give evidence and show the scars they were left to carry for life.

These elementary rights are in marked contrast to the 'justice' given during the 1980s throughout Latin America as military regimes fell one after another across the continent. Unlike in Cuba after the fall of Batista, the new pro-capitalist governments have permitted a conspiracy of silence to take place in order to protect the military and police in their respective countries. Despite hundreds of thousands suffering torture and death, few prosecutions have been made against those responsible for such crimes in Argentina, Chile, Brazil, Peru and other countries. The victims have been denied the opportunity to speak out.

The friends and families of 'los desapparacidos' (the disappeared) rarely get a reply to their simple question carried on placards throughout the continent: *"Donde Están?"* (Where are they?). In Argentina after more than a decade of weekly protests in front of the presidential palace the mothers of the disappeared still ask this same question and still get no reply. Even the bodies of loved ones have not been returned to allow burial and grieving.

The silence of US imperialism about these crimes, in which it and its agencies such as the CIA are directly implicated, has been deafening. It has been in marked contrast to its reaction to the tribunal headed by Che in Cuba.

A gruesome picture was painted by US imperialism of what was taking place in Havana. The 'terror' of the new regime was hypocritically denounced and Che was presented as public enemy number one. The wrath of US imperialism had now been unleashed as the revolution took retribution against the paid lackeys of Washington.

Che was determined to carry through this policy. The wound of recent history was still open and aggravated by his experience during the war. Che repeated endlessly to his Cuban comrades during this period that Arbenz had failed in Guatemala because he failed to purge the armed forces and allowed the CIA to penetrate and overthrow his government. He was determined not to allow history to be repeated in Cuba.

On 22 January a mass rally was called in Havana to support the government's 'war trials' policy. Estimates vary but anything between half a million and one million participated in this mass demonstration. It was bigger than the rally which greeted Castro when he arrived in Havana on 8 January. The revolution was gathering momentum.

Banners denounced US imperialism for its double standards, compared the trials of Batista's assassins with the Nuremberg trials of convicted Nazis after the second world war and demanded 'revolutionary justice'.

Castro asked all those who agreed with revolutionary justice to raise their hands. Up to one million hands were raised to a cry of *"Si"*. Castro commented: *"Gentlemen of the diplomatic corps, gentlemen of the press of the whole continent, the jury of a million Cubans of all ideas and all social classes has voted."*

There was massive support for the measures being taken by the government. Castro was resting on this support and was now mobilising it to answer the attacks and threats from the 'imperialist gringos' in the USA. He was also being pushed along by the pressure of the mass movement which was now gripped with a revolutionary fervour. At the same time the arrogant response and demands of the US compounded this. Within a short space of months the revolution had gone much further than any of its central players had anticipated it would. Even Che had written in 1958: *"... I began the struggle with that spirit: honestly without any hope of going further than the liberation of the country; and fully prepared to leave when the conditions of the struggle veered all the action of the Movement toward the right (toward what all of you represent)."* (*Letter to the July 26th Movement* co-ordinator in the Oriente, 'Daniel').

The Death of Capitalist Cuba

Although Castro was leaning on the masses and defended the 'revolutionary trials' he still was not propagating the idea of a 'socialist revolution'.

All property belonging to Batista and his cronies was taken over by the state during the early days of the revolution. However, Castro was still refuting any 'communist' objectives and declaring his support for the establishment of a capitalist 'democracy' in Cuba.

US imperialism was terrified of the events which were unfolding only 100 miles from its coastline. Though it was justified in its fears, many of its political representatives were also suffering from a severe case of 'communist paranoia' and saw a 'communist plot' in every radical political movement south of the Rio Grande which it did not directly control or influence.

Castro was not trusted but still remained a largely unknown quantity. He was invited to the US by a group of newspaper editors with a view to 'sounding him out'. His visit took place during April and it was evidently intended also as a means of putting pressure on him to follow US wishes. While he was in Washington Castro met, amongst others, Vice-President Richard Nixon for *'discussions'*.

Nixon demanded the end of executions resulting from the 'revolutionary' tribunals and a severing of relations with 'communists'. He presented Castro with a file on 'known communists' in and around his government. Moreover, these demands were linked to the question of economic aid. After the meeting Nixon concluded that Castro was either *"... incredibly naive about communism or was under communist discipline and that we would have to treat him accordingly"*.

'Accordingly', he then supported Federal Bureau of Investigation (FBI) chief, J Edgar Hoover, in urging the US immediately to arm Cuban exiles with a view to overthrowing Castro. The forced removal of Castro became a matter of prestige for the ruling class in the USA and this has determined its policy ever since.

Castro tried to explain to Nixon that any measures his government took against US interests were just and spent the US tour arguing that he was not a communist, that foreign interests would be respected and that his heart was *"in the west"*. For three hours he met with the CIA's 'expert' on communism in Latin America, who concluded: *"Castro is not only not a communist, he is a strong anti-communist."*

US imperialism was not prepared to accept any challenge to its interests in Cuba or throughout the region as a whole. It certainly was not prepared to permit a loosening of its grip in its former playground through the emergence of a more independent, 'national' and 'liberal' reform minded regime in Havana. The result was that Castro, also under pressure from the revolution in Cuba, became locked into a conflict with the USA and capitalism.

Che, during these processes, was urging Castro to go further against capitalism at each stage. The revolution sank deeper and deeper roots and gained momentum. The blows struck against it by US imperialism only served to strengthen it and push it in a still more leftward and socialist direction. In his 1963 article, Building a Party of the Working Class, Che wrote: *"Imperialism has been a very important factor in the development and deepening of our ideology. Each blow dealt by imperialism*

Castro speaks, Havana, 1964

called for a response. Each time the Yankees reacted with their habitual arrogance, by taking some action against Cuba, we had to adopt the necessary counter-measures, and thereby the revolution deepened."

After Castro returned from his American visit a programme of agrarian reform was announced by the government. It had been drafted under Che's influence and its first article proscribed estates larger than 1,000 acres and supported the establishment of co-operatives. Exceptions were allowed and land could even be held by foreign companies if the government deemed it to be in the national interest. In fact this law went little further than the constitution of 1940 but it did allow the government to confiscate land and the new legislation affected about 40% of total farmland.

The land reform programme was to be enacted through the Agrarian Reform Institute, INRA, which appointed farm managers and paid workers $2.50 a day throughout the year. Whilst the proposed agricultural reform may have differed little from the 1940 constitution it was sufficient to arouse the opposition of Cuba's landowners and their friends in the USA from where the spectre of 'Communism in Cuba' was raised.

The price of Cuban sugar on the New York Stock Exchange fell. US companies with investments in Cuba were beginning to panic about whether they would be paid compensation should their assets be taken over by the new government.

The US orchestrated a campaign to oust Castro by demanding he call elections. The response was a massive demonstration of hundreds of thousands of armed Cubans on May Day chanting, *"Revolution Yes Elections No."*

Within Cuba itself a massive radicalisation of workers, poor peasants and youth was taking place alongside a polarisation within the government. Vendors were selling fruit juice on the streets to raise money for the state and the revolution. During the summer of 1959 Castro was still vacillating and speaking of a 'humanist' national revolution which was neither 'capitalist' nor 'communist'.

The openly pro-capitalist 'liberals' in the government lacked any serious figures around which they could rally their limited forces. However, they increasingly protested at the actions of Che in the armed forces and the promotion of known socialists and PSP supporters. They opposed the more radical measures which Castro was agreeing to implement, such as a decree cutting rents by 50% announced in March. An increasing polarisation developed within ruling circles reflecting the pressure of the revolution underway and the series of blows and counter-blows taking place between the USA and Cuba.

President Manuel Urruita was forced to resign in July after massive protests against his opposition to the radical steps being implemented by the government. By November the liberal ministers had been sacked or forced to resign as they joined the Washington chorus against the 'communist' policies of the Cuban government.

Che during these months was demanding still more radical measures. Since January he had been advocating a policy of rapid industrialisation of the economy based upon the nationalisation of mineral wealth, electricity, the telephone company (a subsidiary of the US multi-national ITT) and other sectors of the economy.

Capitalism Snuffed Out

More than anybody else in Cuba, Che now terrified US imperialism with what he was preaching. He anticipated the onslaught from the US government which would follow the adoption of more radical policies. On 27 January he delivered a speech, Social Projections of the Rebel Army. Che proclaimed: *"Our revolution is intimately linked to all the underdeveloped countries of [Latin] America. The revolution is not limited to the Cuban nation because it has touched the conscience of Latin America and seriously alerted the enemies of our peoples. The revolution has put the Latin American tyrants on guard because these are the enemies of popular regimes, as are the monopolistic foreign companies.... Today, all the people of Cuba are on a war footing and should remain so, so that the victory against the dictatorship is not a passing one but becomes the first step to the victory of [Latin] America."*

It was a clarion call to revolutionaries throughout Latin America and a declaration of war against US interests. The US was adopting a policy aimed at strangling the measures being taken by the new regime. The importation of sugar from Cuba was slashed because of the agricultural reform and the nationalisation of foreign petrol companies in June. This followed the importation of Russian oil which US companies in Cuba had refused to refine. The Cuban government appointed administrators at all the refineries owned by Texaco, Esso and Shell and then nationalised them.

Castro retaliated to the cutting of sugar imports with a decree legalising the nationalisation of all foreign assets. In October, 383 large Cuban industries and the banks were taken over by the state. Capitalism was snuffed out. In April 1960, Castro for the first time proclaimed the revolution in Cuba as *"Socialist"*.

A New Cuba

HILST US imperialism was horrified by the events which were taking place in Havana the bureaucratic dictatorship which ruled in Moscow in the name of 'socialism' initially observed events from a distance. The leaders in the Kremlin were, if anything, taken by surprise at the turn events had taken. It is certainly false to assert, as some apologists for the Moscow regime have, that the Cuban revolution was conducted with the support of the USSR from the very beginning and that Castro was collaborating with them.

There had been some limited contact between individual members of the July 26th Movement and Soviet officials in Mexico prior to the Granma expedition. Apart from Raúl Castro's membership of the Young Communists, Che had also had discussions with a Soviet official.

At most, the contact which had taken place was of a fact-finding character. Che, during the time he was in Mexico, saw the Soviet Union as the manifestation of 'socialism'. Moreover, as with many in the colonial and semi-colonial world, the USSR was viewed as an attractive counterweight to imperialism - in Latin America especially US imperialism.

In a letter to 'Daniel' written in 1958, Che had explained that he *"... belonged to those that believe that the solution to the world's problems lies behind the so-called iron curtain..."* Later, as Che was to see Russia at first hand the more critical and hostile he became in his attitude towards the privileged bureaucracy which ruled there in the name of 'socialism' - without losing his hatred of capitalism and imperialism.

If there was a conspiracy involving Castro and the bureaucracy in the Kremlin to take over Cuba then the leaders of the Soviet Union knew nothing about it. As news of the turbulent events in Havana reached Moscow during January 1959, a meeting of the CPSU (Communist Party of the Soviet Union) leaders was taking place. Anderson details events in his Che Guevara biography as they were recalled to him by Giorgi Kornienko, a senior official working in the CPSU Department of Information: *"Khruschchev asked, 'What kind of guys are these? Who are they?' But nobody knew the answer to his question... In reality we didn't know who these guys in Havana were."*

However, once confronted with the social revolution, the Moscow bureaucracy was prepared to step in and use the opportunity which had presented itself. By embracing the Cuban regime under Castro, the Russian leader, Nikita Khrushchev, was able to assert the bureaucracy's international influence and prestige.

This was seen during the Cuban missile crisis in 1962 when, fearing plans for a US intervention, the Cubans appealed for military aid. The Soviet bureaucracy agreed and despatched weapons capable of carrying nuclear warheads. This was done primarily to boost the prestige of the bureaucracy internationally by being seen to 'stand up to' the USA. It was done partly as a tit-for-tat measure against action taken by the USA earlier. By installing nuclear weapons in Cuba Khrushchev argued: *"We can give them back the same medicine they gave us in Turkey [the USA had installed nuclear missiles aimed at the USSR]... It's just to frighten them a bit... They should be made to feel the same way we do... They have to swallow the pill like we swallowed the Turkish one."*

As well as using the situation in Cuba to boost its international prestige, the Russian bureaucracy would also use its influence and economic muscle to control the Cuban leaders who were regarded as wild cards. The bureaucracy which ruled the USSR in 1960 was confident and assertive on the world arena in marked contrast to the demoralised clique who enacted the restoration of capitalism during 1989-92.

Social Gains

Revolutionary Cuba established extremely favourable trading arrangements with the USSR and Eastern Europe. Eighty-five percent of Cuban trade was conducted behind the 'iron curtain' as Cuban sugar was purchased at three and even four times the price on the world market. Ninety-five percent of Cuba's oil was from the USSR. Indeed Russian economic aid amounted in excess of one million US dollars per day. Without such support the Cuban economy and the revolution would have collapsed. As the old saying goes: "He who pays the piper calls the tune". With such dependency the Kremlin had the Castro regime firmly in its grasp.

Investment in industry was undertaken and technicians were sent to Havana. Based upon the overthrow of capitalism and the construction of a planned economy with the economic support of the USSR, the life of the Cuban masses was transformed.The gains made as a consequence of the revolution contrasted with the 'free market' sea of misery in which the rest of the population on the continent was left to drown.

Within two years illiteracy was abolished. Prior to 1959, fifty percent of children of primary school age received no education at all; after the revolution it was available to all. Teachers and students were sent to organise classes in the factories and on the farms. When everybody in the workplace could read and write a red flag was flown at the entrance. Health care was developed and made freely available to everybody. Eventually it would rank amongst the best in the world. Work, food and housing were available for all. Infant mortality was reduced to 10.6 per thousand and life expectancy increased to 74 years by the late 1970s. These age expectancy levels compared favourably to the major imperialist countries. It compared at the time to 45 years in Bolivia, about 60 in Brazil and 58 in Colombia.

Castro's government was the first on the continent to openly proclaim its allegiance to 'socialism'. Earlier inclusion of the socialist or communist parties in governments in Latin America had been through coalition with a variety of capitalist parties. Any adherence to building socialism rapidly faded and was dropped. Not until Allende's election in Chile in 1970 was another Latin American government to proclaim its intention of building socialism.

Moreover, the victory in Cuba was achieved by revolution. The effect throughout the continent was electric. Workers, peasants and youth throughout Latin America began to look to Cuba as an example which they aspired to emulate. Cuba was now a beacon to the exploited masses of Latin America. The enthusiasm which events in Havana had generated further south was only mirrored by the horror with which they were greeted by the capitalist rulers north of the Rio Grande.

Bay of Pigs

From what José Martí described as *"inside the monster"* of US imperialism plans were laid to overthrow Castro's 'Communist threat'. In April 1961 planes from the US bombed the city of Santiago de Cuba. It was in response to this attack that

Major social gains - the abolition of illiteracy and education available for all

Castro proclaimed the "socialist character" of the revolution. This attack was a prelude to an invasion in the same month at Playa Girón (Bay of Pigs) by US organised mercenary forces. The assault collapsed into a farce as the US pulled back from an all-out attack on Cuban soil and was repelled by armed militias.

Each attempted assault by US imperialism merely served to strengthen support for the revolution and Castro's regime. Che, with justification, sent a written message to President john F Kennedy after the invasion at Playa Girón: *"Thank you for Playa Girón. Before the invasion, the revolution was shaky. Now, it is stronger than ever."*

The failure of this invasion was then followed by a campaign to isolate Cuba internationally. The expulsion of Cuba from the Organisation of American States (OAS) was carried out on 31 January 1962. This was followed by a total US trade embargo which still exists today.

On 4 February Castro hit back in a lengthy speech, *The Second Declaration of Havana*. It was delivered to an audience of one million - one in seven of the entire population. It was an outstanding summary of the history of Latin America, denouncing capitalism and imperialism and calling for revolution and socialism throughout the continent.

Castro was more than justified in proclaiming: *"Cuba, the Latin American nation which has made landowners of more than 100,000 small farmers, ensured employment all the year on state farms and co-operatives to all agricultural workers, transformed forts into schools, given 70,000 scholarships to university, secondary and technological students, created lecture halls for the entire child population, totally liquidating illiteracy, quadrupling medical services, nationalising foreign interests, suppressing the abusive system which turned housing into a means of exploiting people, virtually eliminating unemployment, suppressing discrimination due to race or sex, ridding itself of gambling vice and administrative corruption, armed the people... is expelled from the Organisation of American States by governments which have not achieved for their people one of these objectives."*

Referring to the wrath aroused amongst the defenders of capitalism the declaration argued: *"What explains it is fear. Not fear of the Cuban revolution but fear of the Latin American revolution...fear that the workers, peasants, students, intellectuals and progressive sectors of the middle strata will by revolutionary means take power in the oppressed and hungry countries exploited by the Yankee monopolies and reactionary oligarchies of America, fear that the plundered people of the continent will seize arms from their oppressors and, like Cuba, declare themselves free people of America."*

The achievements of the Cuban revolution together with such declarations ensured that it won massive support at home and abroad. However, despite the popularity of the new regime and the tremendous gains made by the revolution, it did not result in the establishment of a genuine system of workers' democracy.

The Russian Revolution, 1917

A New Cuba but Run by Whom?

After the Russian revolution in 1917 a system of workers' democracy was established through the election of soviets (councils). These comprised delegates elected from the factories, workplaces and military units. Similar forms of organisation have been established by the working class in other revolutions, including during the Paris Commune which was established in 1871. After the Russian revolution the local soviets would elect regional and national councils from which the government was formed.

All those delegates elected could be replaced by those who elected them at any time. Government officials were paid no more than the average wage of skilled workers. Lenin argued the maximum differential in wages and salaries should be four to one. Through this system of workers' democracy the working class, with the support of the poor peasants and other exploited layers, exercised democratic control and management over the running and planning of society.

As a result the Russian revolution had a massive impact internationally. It was as John Reed entitled his vibrant account of the revolution *Ten Days that Shook the World*. Workers world wide not only supported the revolution but they fought to emulate a similar system of workers' democracy in their own countries. It had an even bigger and more practical impact internationally than the sympathy which was aroused by the Cuban revolution.

The system of workers' democracy which was established during the Russian revolution was built on the basis of the working class consciously taking over the running of society. With the proletariat at the head of the revolutionary process a workers' state was established which reflected the class character of the revolution. It was this which had such an impact on workers throughout the world.

The working class eventually lost political power to a bureaucratic elite because of the failure of the international revolution and the military intervention by 21 armies of imperialism which strengthened counter-revolutionary forces in Russia. The civil war which raged between 1918 and 1921 resulted in an horrific economic and social catastrophe. Because of the starvation which developed in rural areas even cannibalism took place. These events and the failure of the victory of the revolution internationally eventually exhausted the working class, especially the most politically active and experienced workers. A privileged and bureaucratic caste emerged which took political power. A repressive bureaucratic regime ruled in the name of 'socialism' until 1989/91.

In Cuba the new regime which came to power in 1959 was tremendously popular and enjoyed massive support amongst the population. But the character of the state which was established reflected the predominately rural and peasant basis of the revolution. As a result a workers' democracy similar to that which took power in Russia in 1917 was not established.

Despite its support and popularity the Cuban regime was from the beginning not a workers' democracy but what the Committee for a Workers' International (CWI) would characterise as a deformed workers' state. That is to say a state where capitalism and landlordism were overthrown and replaced with a state- owned planned economy but run and controlled by a bureaucratic caste. There was no system of soviets or workers' councils through which the proletariat could govern society.

The government would rule mainly through the Communist Party and the Committees for the Defence of the Revolution (CDRs) which the new regime formed in September 1960. These were not elected bodies based upon the workplaces through which the working class could initiate proposals or revise and amend those coming from regional and national level. This is essential to allow a centrally planned economy to develop most effectively and exercise a check over bureaucratic tendencies.

Every street had a CDR which anyone could initially join and they consequently boasted three million members. These acted as a transmission belt for the decisions of the government which were communicated to them mainly through members of the Communist Party. They functioned as the mechanism through which the party leadership conducted local plebiscites to endorse its decisions. There was no effective channel through which the workers and the population could debate and change the decisions taken above.

This method of rule was frequently used by Castro. Mass rallies were called and proposals presented to those in attendance who were asked to endorse them 'Si' or 'no'. There was no debate or discussion or check and control.

In the fervour of the early days of the revolution, through the CDRs, an element of control was exercised largely on day-to-day issues. However, they have never functioned as a mechanism through which the democratic planning and control of the economy and society as a whole could be carried out by the working class. Although they were popular in the early period of the revolution amongst many workers they increasingly played the role of informing on the activities of the local population.

The trade unions, through the CTC, rapidly became little more than the supervisory agency for the relevant government ministry.There also existed nearly 300 municipal councils but they had little power. Candidates all had to fulfil the criteria laid down by the party which also appointed the presidents.

The Cuban Communist Party remains the main instrument through which the bureaucracy conducts its rule. The party itself is run on the basis of appointments made at each level from the top down. It was formally established in 1965 on a controlled basis following a purge which had taken place in the ORI (Integrated Revolutionary Organisations) of all PSP members who had participated in the rigged elections Batista called in 1958.

With 70,000 members in 1969 it was proportionally the smallest of the 'communist parties' per head of population of the so-called 'communist' countries. Its members were hand-picked by commissions which were appointed by the party's Central Committee and factions were outlawed. Commissions of "exemplary" workers and especially technicians from the workplaces were selected. Despite being formed in 1965 the Communist Party only held its first congress in 1975. Other political parties were banned.

In Russia even during the conditions of civil war the Bolshevik party held a congress every year. Under Lenin and Trotsky factions within the party were banned (Lenin wanted this as a temporary measure) when the revolution was threatened by the civil war and imperialist intervention from 21 countries. Other parties were only banned when they resorted to taking up arms against the revolution and collaborated with imperialist intervention.

Bureaucratic Planning

A central planning mechanism was established firstly through INRA and then JUCEPLAN which was an imitation of the bureaucratic planning mechanisms which existed in the USSR. Che played a leading role in both and was head of the nationalised Cuban National Bank.

'Advisers' from behind the 'iron curtain' arrived and increasingly influenced the centralised planning mechanism. By 1961 more than 100 Eastern European 'advisers' were in Havana. The masses were not in control of the central or local planning of the economy. The bureaucratic control of the economy resulted in a series of economic 'zigzags' and unrealisable targets being set as the regime attempted to overcome shortages and problems. In 1960 Castro promised that living standards equal to Sweden would be achieved by 1965. In 1961 Che Guevara declared that Cuba would become an industrialised country within twelve months. The same year food rationing was introduced which was continued right up until the 1970s!

The excessive targets and zigzags were pronounced in the important agricultural sector as well as in industry. In countries like Cuba a harmonious development of agriculture and industry is essential. A high degree of industrial development and mechanisation is necessary in order to boost agricultural production to the maximum. This requires a finely tuned correlation being established between industry and agriculture. It is not possible to achieve this without a system of workers' democracy - and where there is a bureaucracy ruling society from the top. Trotsky argued this case in his criticism of Stalin's agricultural policies in the 1930s.

Castro declared in the late 1960s that Cuban sugar production would reach ten million tons by 1970. This would only have been possible with the development of industry and mechanisation of agriculture. Only eight million tons were harvested in 1970 and 5.4 million in 1975. In a desperate race to meet the 1970 target 400,000 Cubans were mobilised from the cities to reap the harvest. This policy of the mass mobilisation of voluntary labour (at times forced labour) was an attempt to provide a substitute for the lack of mechanisation. In turn it resulted in a dislocation of production in the cities and added to the problems which existed in industry.

Che and Castro attempted to resolve some of the economic difficulties which arose because of the bureaucracy. They bemoaned the symptoms but could not find a cure. Even in 1963 Che was having to deal with problems which were arising because of the system of bureaucratic rule. He delivered a secret speech which was "for the private use of political and economic leaders" in which he castigated managers for the poor quality of goods. However, to cure the desease of bureaucracy a system of workers' democracy which permitted criticism of decision makers and the discussion and changes of plans was necessary. This was absent in Cuba.

In a small country like Cuba, the difficulties which would even be encountered by a regime of workers' democracy would demand the victory of the socialist revolution internationally - especially throughout Latin America in order to obtain the necessary resources and technique through the integration and planning of the economies throughout the continent. That is why the struggle for a socialist federation of Latin America is of such crucial importance for the working class and exploited peoples of the continent.

Che supported and fought for the victory of such an international revolution.

Unfortunately the ideas he advocated to achieve it did not correspond to the conditions which existed in other more urbanised countries of Latin America.

The bureaucratic influence of the USSR worsened the situation. At central level it attempted to impose its own budgeting system. This ludicrous policy meant that each industry financially operated separately irrespective of the national accounts. One industry could not therefore offer subsidies to another even when this was economically desirable. Che resisted attempts to impose this in Cuba. Other aspects of Russian 'aid' were almost comical if not tragic. Houses designed for the sub-zero conditions in Serbia were built in sun soaked Cuba! A thousand Russian tractors were sent in 1963 to harvest sugar cane. Once unloaded it was discovered they could not be used for the task as special machinery was required.

Wage differentials existed from the outset of the new regime. K S Carol remarks in his book, *Guerrillas in Power*, that by 1963 he had encountered an engineer in one factory who received 17 times the wage of a worker. It was a long way from Lenin's proposed maximum differential of four to one.

The Cuban bureaucracy took privileges for itself although because of the backwardness of Cuba these appeared less than those taken by the bureaucrats in the Kremlin. However, they are no less significant in social measurements. In 1975 the Communist Party congress voted to allow Cubans to buy cars. Until then this had been the preserve of party and state officials. During the food rationing of 1961 government officials were given higher rations than workers and peasants. At the same time better quality and more expensive restaurants like 'Torre' and '1830' were frequented by party and government officials. For workers they remained inaccessible.

Not For Che

Some of these privileges were literally taken from what the rich had left behind as they fled Cuba. Che was not to be a party to such activities and was repelled by them. He grew increasingly irritated by the bureaucratic features which were emerging in the new Cuba.

Orlando Borrego worked with Che in JUCEPLAN and recalls one incident. Having 'intervened' in a sugar mill Borrego had taken a brand new Jaguar car which the former owner had left behind and drove around in it for a week. Che spotted him and ran to him yelling: *"You're a pimp. It is a pimp's car. Not one representative of the people should be driving it, get rid of it. You have two hours."* Borrego recalls *"Che was super strict...like Jesus Christ."*

He rejected privileges for himself and lived a frugal lifestyle. As head of the National Bank he refused the higher salary to which he was entitled and insisted on living on the minimal wage paid to a 'comandante'. When food rationing was

Che, setting an example - Working on Havana's Docks, 1961

introduced in 1961 he was appalled to find out by accident that his ration was higher than that being given to the mass of the population and immediately cut it accordingly.

He even refused to use government petrol allocated for official duties to take his wife to hospital and wanted his father and family to pay their own air fare from Argentina when they visited him in Cuba. His commitment to the revolution and his life style earned him a special place in the hearts of the Cuban and Latin American masses.

Increasingly, Che reacted with hostility to what he saw in the Soviet Union. On one visit, invited to dinner in the apartment of a government official, he ate his meal on the finest imported French porcelain. During the dinner he turned to his host and sarcastically quipped: *"So, the proletariat here eats off French porcelain, eh?"*

Back in Cuba he grew frustrated by the quality of the industrial supplies sent from Moscow which he denounced as *"horse shit"*. On one occasion, when suffering from a particularly bad attack of asthma, he was visited by his friend, Padilla, who, having just returned from the USSR, was denouncing what he had seen. Che interrupted him: *"I must tell you I don't need to listen to what you have to say because I already know all of that is a pigsty, I saw it myself."*

Although repelled by what he saw in the USSR and frustrated by the emerging bureaucratic methods and mistakes in Cuba, Che had no clear alternative. His central weakness, the lack of an understanding of the role of the working class in the revolution and in consciously planning and running society, now prevented him from developing a viable alternative policy.

To this must be added his lack of any worked out explanation about the Stalinist states in the USSR and Eastern Europe. From a Marxist point of view, both of these deficiencies in his ideas would conspire against him. He correctly looked to extend the revolution beyond Cuba's borders but failed to grasp how this could be done.

International Policy

All he could offer was an appeal to repeat the revolution and its methods of 'guerrillaism'. Because of the authority of the Cuban revolution this had a big impact on layers of youth and intellectuals throughout Latin America and Europe. However, despite sympathising with the Cuban revolution and Che, this method of struggle was not viewed as viable to the powerful working class which was growing up in Chile, Argentina, Brazil, Bolivia and other countries. Che failed to turn to this powerful and potentially revolutionary class and offer it an alternative revolutionary socialist programme to the policies of class collaboration, reformism and popular frontism which were on offer from the socialist and communist parties in the region.

Che's ideas on internationalism had mass support in Cuba and the new regime was prepared to echo them as a counter-weight to the vicious blockade by imperialism. Under Che's influence the regime supported and initiated guerrilla organisations in numerous countries.

This was tolerated for a brief time by the bureaucracy in the USSR despite causing it some problems in its dealings with local communist parties which rejected these methods. Conflicts and disagreements also took place between Havana and Moscow. From the Kremlin's point of view it was a price worth paying as the economic aid Moscow was giving to Cuba strengthened its international prestige especially in the colonial and semi-colonial countries.

Although the support of the Castro regime to numerous guerrilla forces in Latin America was a source of irritation to the Moscow bureaucracy, it was not threatened by it. It could tolerate it for a period of time and even use it to its own advantage against US imperialism. The different attitude shown by Khrushchev towards the events in Hungary in 1956 and those which developed in Cuba illustrated the nature of the regime in Havana.

In the Hungarian uprising in 1956 workers' councils were formed. Power was in the hands of the working class and the masses which posed a mortal threat to the bureaucracy. A victorious revolution in Hungary would threaten to spread in a series of uprisings to Eastern Europe and the USSR. The bureaucracy would not compromise with this threat. Khrushchev drowned the Hungarian revolution in blood.

However, to Havana he extended the hand of friendship in the form of trade agreements and aid because the nature of the Castro regime did not threaten the rule of the bureaucrats in the Kremlin.

International policy reflects domestic policy. By 1968, after Che's death, Havana attempted to soften its relations with US imperialism and its cohorts in Latin America. This reflected the Cuban bureaucracy's consolidation of power and a temporary easing of the trade boycott by the USA. Cuban support to revolutionary movements internationally lessened. The interests of the national regime had a higher priority than the international revolutionary movement.

The Mexican government was the only capitalist state to keep diplomatic relations with Havana. It acted as a messenger service between Havana and Washington as it does today. In Mexico in October 1968 the military massacred up to 1,000 students. Not a word of protest emanated from the Cuban Communist Party or the government.

Moreover, there was a marked contradiction in the policy Cuba adopted towards the guerrilla movements and the struggles of the working class. As workers' movements erupted during the stormy decade of the 1960s Castro and the Cuban regime were notably silent.

When European capitalism was shaken by the general strike of ten million workers in France during May 1968 there was silence from Havana. In the same year Castro supported the military intervention of the Russian bureaucracy into Czechoslovakia.

Congo to Bolivia

THE INTERNATIONALIST spirit of Che had a big impact on young Cuban people. Delegations of youth arrived to see him and sent letters pleading to be allowed to go and fight in Nicaragua, Guatemala, the Dominican Republic, Venezuela and other countries. A special government department was established, Liberación, with responsibility *"for the Latin American revolution".*

Foreign policy is a continuation of domestic policy and, like the CDRs, the international departments of Cuba's government had two sides. To begin with those involved were usually motivated with the desire to spread the revolution and lend assistance to fighters in other countries. Refuge was offered to those throughout the region who were persecuted and had nowhere else to go.

However, the support Liberación offered was almost entirely directed to guerrilla organisations and not orientated to the working class. Guerrilla groups were trained and resources channelled to them. Che was involved in assisting groups from Guatemala, Peru, Venezuela and Nicaragua. Many of the leaders of the Nicaraguan FSLN, such as Tomás Borge and Rodolfo Romero, who were members of the Sandinista leadership which took power in 1979, went through training in Cuba.

This early support, reflecting the role of the Castro regime, later became the instrument to exercise control and to impose Havana's desired policy over various guerrilla and left-wing groups. Increasingly this was done to meet the needs of the bureaucracy in Moscow.

This was later illustrated when the Sandinistas seized power in a similar process to that which unfolded in Cuba. However, they did not then proceed to nationalise the decisive sectors of the economy and overthrow capitalism.

During 1985, under the threat of counter-revolution backed from the US, the Sandinista leaders were flirting with the idea of *'doing a Cuba'.* In April, Sandinista leader Daniel Ortega visited Moscow to discuss getting the support of the Soviet bureaucracy. Unwilling to become embroiled in a war in Central America and with different interests and a changed international situation compared to that which existed in 1959/60, the Moscow bureaucracy declined giving its support.

Castro dutifully supported his paymasters and put pressure on the FSLN leaders. A small number of Soviet MIG fighter planes destined for Nicaragua were impounded in Havana. He had previously visited the Nicaraguan capital, Managua, in January 1985 to urge the FSLN to support a mixed economy, telling them: *"You can have a capitalist economy"* and praised Ortega for his *"serious and responsible approach".*

Che in the early 1960s was intent on developing the revolution by the application of his guerrilla methods throughout the South American continent. In particular he hoped for a revolutionary upsurge in his native Argentina.

Castro wanted to strengthen his regime and win the support of Khrushchev. After returning from Moscow during 1963 with vast economic aid from the USSR, he was less concerned with the idea of spreading the revolution beyond Cuba's shores and declared that he was *"ready to do whatever is necessary to establish good neighbourly relations with the United States of America, based upon the principles of coexistence".*

A guerrilla operation was initiated in Argentina during 1962 by the Ejército Guerrillero del Pueblo (People's Guerrilla Army). With its massive urban working class it was the least applicable country to launch a guerrilla war. The offensive was undertaken to coincide with the second anniversary of the military taking power. It was a disaster and the group was slaughtered, including two of his closest collaborators, Hermes Pena and Jorge Ricardo Masetti.

The episode had a devastating effect on Che. *"... Here you see me behind a desk, fucked, while my people die during missions I've sent them on,"* he replied when asked why he was appearing depressed.

A combination of this and other defeats for guerrilla forces internationally, alongside frustration at the growing bureaucratisation of the Cuban regime had led him to decide he should return to the battlefield. He finally left Cuba during 1965 and went not to Latin America but to Africa and fought in the Congo. Ever since the overthrow of Patrice Lumumba's government and his assassination the Congo had been at the centre of an important conflict with imperialism.

The Congo Disaster

Che left a letter to Castro, praising his qualities as a *"revolutionary leader"* and absolving Cuba of any of his future actions. Typically he wrote: *"... I am not sorry that I leave nothing material to my wife and children. I am happy it is that way. I ask nothing for them, as the state will provide them with enough to live on and to have an education..."*

He finished the text with his famous phrase which was to become a battle cry of the youth throughout Latin America in the struggle against the dictatorships which imprisoned the continent during the 1970s and 1980s, *"Hasta la victoria siempre!"* (Always until victory).

However, the hopes and aspirations with which he departed for the Congo with a force of Cubans were rapidly dashed. The mission was to turn into a disaster and result in defeat. It was ill-prepared and undertaken almost as an act of desperation. Moreover, it was a mission which was imposed from outside. As Che admitted later the Congolese knew little of it until he arrived in their country.

When his forces reached Dar-Es-Salaam, Tanzania, where the rebel leaders were based, none could be found. They were abroad in Cairo. Amongst them was Laurent Kabila who over thirty years later would take power in the Congo.

The Cuban forces were shocked by what they found amongst the rebel army. Not only did it lack any coherent political direction but was in Che's words *"a parasitic army"*. The local peasants were terrified of it. Soldiers would rob them and assault the women. In the conflicts witnessed by Che the fighters would usually flee from battle. Officers would often lead drunken binges followed by fights. Kabila was seen by Cubans driving around Dar-Es-Salaam in a Mercedes Benz and was never present when battles were imminent.

All of this was in marked contrast to what the Cuban forces were used to and expected. Eventually they were compelled to withdraw and admit defeat following an assault by government forces on the rebels. Che found refuge in the Cuban embassy in Tanzania and via Eastern Europe eventually returned clandestinely to Cuba. However, having built his reputation on fighting to the end he could not return to Havana 'empty handed'.

Onto Bolivia and Death

Che's aim was to return to his homeland of Argentina and continue the struggle there but this proved to be impossible. In 1967 he emerged in Bolivia with the view of igniting a revolutionary movement through a guerrilla campaign. From this he hoped to radiate to the surrounding countries a series of revolutionary struggles. It was an heroic gesture, like much of Che's political struggle. Like the Congo, it turned out to be another adventure, this time with fatal consequences for him. An iron law of history, that revolution cannot be artificially imposed from the outside, was illustrated in a tragic manner.

Although Bolivia had a bigger rural population than Argentina it had a strong working class spearheaded by the revolutionary traditions of the tin miners. This was ignored by Che despite his having witnessed the mass revolutionary upsurge of 1953. Moreover, an extensive programme of land reform was carried out during the Bolivian revolution in the 1950s. This made the peasantry less inclined and receptive to take up an armed struggle and lend support to a guerrilla army.

As his plans were laid for this campaign, Che failed to win the active support of the Bolivian Communist Party (PCB) which initially, at least formally, took a neutral stand and even allowed some of its members to help with preparations for the campaign.

Havana Airport, March 15, 1965 - After returning to Cuba following open criticism of Moscow's lack of support for socialist revolution. Immediately afterwards, Fidel proposed to Che that he lead a Cuban expeditionary force to the Congo

In part this was to allow its leadership to appear more 'revolutionary' as it feared being outflanked on the left. It was especially fearful of the Trotskyist party, the POR (Workers' Revolutionary Party), which had a powerful tradition and semi-mass influence in the country, especially amongst the tin miners.

In reality the PCB failed to organise support for the guerrilla force and its leaders were very sceptical about supporting such methods. Mario Monje and the other leaders certainly did not want a guerrilla campaign being fought in their own backyard. The party was still wedded to the idea of coalition with the 'progressive' sections of the national bourgeoisie.

Castro had agreed with Monje and other PCB leaders that they should have the monopoly on political and material support. In reality the PCB leadership provided little back-up to Che's forces. This was partly because of the situation in Bolivia.

There were also international factors which bore down on Monje and the PCB leadership. The Moscow bureaucracy wanted to rein in the guerrilla movements which were adding to the instability developing in Latin America. The Cuban regime was seen to be encouraging them and its activities needed to be 'controlled'. Che was regarded as an irresponsible adventurer in the Kremlin. He was denounced as a 'Trotskyist' and a 'Maoist' amongst circles in the Kremlin.

This was manifested at an international conference which took place in January 1966, the so-called Tri-Continental Conference. This event took place in Havana and was attended by delegates from Asia, Africa and Latin America as well as China and Russia. Apart from government representatives, guerrilla groups were present, mainly from Latin America. Here Castro attracted the attention of the Chinese bureaucracy whose interests conflicted with their counterparts in the USSR.

At the same time Castro pushed through a resolution supporting guerrilla movements - much to the annoyance of the Moscow leaders. Monje made a rapid visit to Moscow after the conference. Arising from discussions he had with CPSU officials he concluded that they, like him, saw Che as the driving force behind this policy - although he was not present at the conference.

According to Monje he was urged by CPSU officials to stand up to the Cubans and not to be pushed around by them. Monje was certainly encouraged by the bureaucracy not to mobilise the PCB in support of Che's guerrilla operation.

This and the friction which existed between the PCB leaders and Che was known in Havana when Castro agreed to give the PCB a monopoly on political and practical support to Che and his guerrillas.

In the event, Che launched his crusade in one of the most isolated areas of Bolivia, in the south east of the country, 250 kilometres south of Santa Cruz. His guerrilla force was named the ELN (National Liberation Army). At its peak his forces numbered 29 Bolivians and 18 Cubans. The area chosen to launch the offensive was one of the least populated with no tradition of struggle amongst the local peasants. Not surprisingly, Che's expedition failed to gain any local support. The failure of Che's forces to win any real local basis also reflected that after the land reform enacted during the revolution of 1953 the peasants were not disposed to take to the road of armed struggle.

After months of fighting the guerrilla force was isolated and suffered setback after setback. Che's health began to give out and he was forced to ride on horseback, unable to walk because of asthma attacks. No support was forthcoming from Havana and communications with the ELN broke down.

It is safe to assume that the Moscow bureaucracy wanted Che 'out of the way'. Castro remained passive as one of the principal leaders of the Cuban revolution faced his final months and weeks. Regis Debray, who was in Bolivia with Che Guevara, has since moved to the right politically and became an adviser to Francois Mitterrand, the ex-French president. During 1996 he attacked Castro and Havana accusing them of abandoning Che and his forces.

Che's small force was in battle against 1,500 soldiers from the Bolivian army. In collaboration with the CIA they tracked his forces down. After a hopeless engagement on 8 October he and his guerrillas were captured near the village of La Higuera, east of Sucre.

The next day he was interviewed for forty five minutes by Lieutenant Colonel Andres Selich, after which his murder was ordered by Cuban-born CIA agent, Felix Rodriquez. He lay bound hand and foot next to the bodies of two dead guerrilla fighters. When asked, *"Are you Cuban or Argentinean?"* Che replied: *"I am Cuban,*

Argentinean, Bolivian, Peruvian, Ecuadorian, etc... You understand."

He was executed at the age of 39 and buried in a secret grave which has been discovered. His body has now been returned to Cuba. His executioners cut off his hands after his death and sent them back to Havana as proof of his death.

Painted on a wall near his grave in Bolivia is a simple slogan: *"Che - Alive as they never wanted you to be."* The spirit of an heroic commitment to struggle against oppression has been bequeathed to new generations. His example still inspires many to struggle to overthrow capitalism and fight for a socialist alternative. Three decades after his death, Marxists can salute Che as an honest and heroic revolutionary.

The tragedy of Che was that his heroism was not linked with a fully rounded-out programme and ideas which could bring about the objective he aspired to - an international socialist revolution. The necessity of achieving this is more urgent than ever. It will be accomplished if today's revolutionaries learn from the experience of Che Guevara's struggle and emulate his audacity and self-sacrifice in the struggle to bring about a socialist society.

Epilogue

THREE DECADES after Che's death Cuba is once again at a crossroads. Against the background of a transformed international situation the threat of counter-revolution and capitalist restoration threatens. US imperialism has once again tightened its grip and is spearheading attempts to overthrow Castro and recapture a playground for business tycoons

With the loss of favourable trading arrangements with the former USSR in 1990/91 Cuba was plunged into economic crisis. This has been compounded by the attempts of US imperialism to isolate Cuba with the imposition of a trade embargo aimed at strangling the economy.

Every US President since the Cuban revolution in 1959 has attempted to take measures aimed at bringing about the downfall of the Castro regime and restoring capitalism. Apart from economic blockades and sponsoring mercenary forces other notable efforts by the CIA have included sending exploding cigars to "el jefe maximo" in Havana.

Castro, much to the irritation of the occupants of the White House, has survived nine US Presidents, each of whom underestimated the massive support which existed in Cuba for the revolution - despite the absence of a genuine regime of workers' democracy.

However, the past gains of the Cuban revolution are now under threat as the prospect of capitalist restoration looms as a likely prospect. The regime, confronting the loss of economic support from the former USSR and isolation, has been driven to adopt a new economic policy. This has opened it up to foreign investment and ownership of sections of the economy, legalised the circulation of the US dollar and begun to threaten the existence of a centrally planned economy.

Prior to 1990/91 trade with the former regimes in the USSR and Eastern Europe accounted for 85% of Cuban exports. Sugar exports subsequently fell by 70%. The loss of these outlets and subsidies from these regimes resulted in a plummeting of the economy. Cuban gross domestic product nose-dived by more than 30% during 1991. Despite apparently stabilising the decline and increasing production during the last two years, the collapse which occurred during the early 1990s has not been made up for.

Living standards fell dramatically and the rationing of bread and rice was introduced. Rationalisation in the state sector led to the laying off of up to 500,000 workers. The regime has taken measures to ensure that health care and education are defended but has been unable to prevent the return of some of the worst aspects of life under capitalism. Although not on the scale which existed prior to the revolution, prostitution has returned to the streets of Havana.

In a desperate attempt to stop the economic collapse the regime was forced to take steps to attract foreign investment and acquire access to the international markets.The 100% foreign ownership of some industries has now been legalised.

Imperialism Divided

This change in policy by Castro's government has opened up a division amongst the contending imperialist powers.

European (especially Spanish), Canadian and Japanese imperialism have sought to take advantage of this situation. They have encouraged investment in the Cuban economy. Canada is now Cuba's leading trade and investment partner followed by Spain. By 1996 there were an estimated 650 foreign companies with investments in Cuba. Other more powerful Latin American capitalist countries, such as Mexico and Brazil, have followed suit with a view to extending their economic and political influence in the region.

Apart from taking economic advantage of the opening, through this policy they hope to pressurise the bureaucracy to move towards capitalism and disperse the planned economy. They are implementing this policy with a view to marrying the bureaucracy, or sections of it, together with capitalism and converting it into a capitalist class together with sections of the exile Cuban population in Florida.

This policy has been tremendously complicated because of the attitude of US imperialism which has adopted a more aggressive and confrontational approach. This has been to try and 'starve out' Castro and overthrow his regime and install their loyal Cuban backers from Miami.

It is a shortsighted policy but reflects the different pressures which US imperialism is under. It has been fuelled by historical considerations, of avenging the damaged prestige of US imperialism which lost its playground to Castro in 1959.

It has also been determined by the need of consecutive US administrations to gain the support of the 700,000 Cubans living in Florida. The Cuban-American National Foundation, one of the most powerful lobby groups in Washington, had a decisive effect in enacting the Helms-Burton Act, which tightened the embargo on Cuba and even penalised foreign companies which invested in the country.

Other reactionary, if smaller, groups like Alpha 66 have attempted terrorist and armed actions against the Castro regime. Whilst within this there is a body of 'moderate' opinion which would support a compromise with the Castro regime there is also a powerful reactionary force of former Cuban capitalists and their dependants.

These forces are in no mood to compromise with the Castro bureaucracy and seek to reclaim factories and land which they lost during the course of the revolution. Should they return to Cuba many would do so with the intention of wreaking their revenge.

The stance of US imperialism, together with the threat of the Cuban exiles, has created big obstacles to those sections of the Cuban bureaucracy which would be more enthusiastic about embracing capitalism and attempting to convert itself into a capitalist class. This is an important difference with the events which developed in the former USSR and Eastern Europe. The bureaucracy in those countries had the prospect of themselves becoming the ruling class (The exception was Eastern Germany where the old bureaucracy was largely pensioned off by West German imperialism.)

The enthusiasm for the revolution and hatred of US imperialism has enabled the leadership of the Cuban regime, especially Castro, to maintain massive support in Cuba despite the economic collapse which has taken place since 1990. The aggressive arrogance of US imperialism has rebounded on it and helped to maintain the Cuban leadership in power.

However, the Cuban government has been compelled to move in the direction of taking pro-capitalist measures and to try and secure the investment of the non-US imperialist powers. These accelerated during 1993/94 and foreign ownership was allowed in tourism and some other sectors.

Even agriculture was affected. In 1992, 75% of Cuba's cultivable land was under the control of state farms which enjoyed massive subsidies. By 1995 this figure had fallen to 27% - the rest being farmed by private co-operatives which lease land from the government and buy equipment. A fixed quota must be sold to the state and anything above this can be sold privately.

These and other measures have allowed a certain growth in the economy to take place in the last two years but it has not made up anything like what was lost after 1991. These same policies have also led to the growth of inequalities. Workers employed in joint ventures, partly or wholly owned by foreign companies, are paid higher wages - in dollars which were legally allowed in circulation in 1993. A black market has inevitably developed under these conditions.

When implementing these measures Castro has presented them as temporary steps forced upon the regime because of the situation. At the same time he has proclaimed his continued support for socialism. When agreeing to open the economy to foreign investment, the policy was "... *not being inspired by neo-liberalism nor does it aim for a transition to capitalism. It is an opening to defend and develop socialism and this is not concealed by our government."*

The apparent defence by Castro of the revolution and 'socialism' in the face of imperialist aggression from the USA has reinforced support for Cuba in the minds of many youth and workers internationally during the last five years. For many Cuba is now seen as the only regime which is still defending socialism and fighting the threat of imperialist aggression and capitalist restoration.

The international workers' movement has a responsibility to oppose all aggression by imperialism and attempts to restore capitalism in Cuba. At the same time it is necessary to see what lies behind the defence of 'socialism' by Castro and the Cuban bureaucracy.

A section of it is resisting attempts to move towards capitalist restoration. In part this is because it does not want to abandon the social gains conquered by the revolution and preside over the misery and chaos which a return to capitalism would mean in Cuba.

Most importantly, because of the reaction of US imperialism and the threat posed by a returning exile capitalist class to sections of the Cuban bureaucracy, the latter has been compelled to try and avoid a return to capitalism in order to protect its own interests and privileges.

The bureaucracy has been forced verbally to defend the revolution and oppose imperialism as a means of trying to maintain and rest upon a basis of support amongst the masses. At the same time it is determined to maintain its rule and control over society. This is reflected in the continuation of a one-party state. The Cuban Communist Party is the instrument through which the bureaucracy controls society.

Friends of Socialism?

Notwithstanding Castro's defence of 'socialism' the other side of his dual policy has been to secure investment from other imperialist countries outside the USA. With their money has also come capitalist politicians and ideas. The hated pro-Thatcherite former Spanish minister, Carlos Solchaga, was invited to Havana as an economics adviser. Castro declared his desire to meet Margaret Thatcher in person and has already met with the Pope as part of a clear overture to the Catholic Church.

In an ironical repetition of history, as in 1968 (when the Mexican military slaughtered a thousand students) the Cuban government and Communist Party remained virtually silent about the uprising of the indigenous people in Chiapas, Mexico. No support was offered to the heroic battles of the Mexican bus and petrol workers to their fight against privatisation.

International policy still reflects domestic policy and the interests of the Cuban

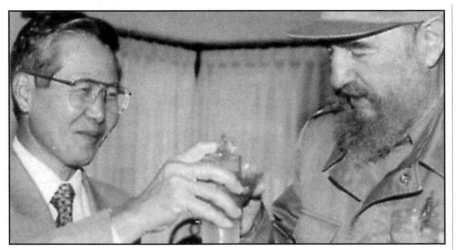

Castro with Peruvian President Fujimori, Havana

regime. It cannot be a coincidence that the silence from Havana regarding the struggles of the Mexican masses is at a time when Mexican capitalism is amongst the largest investors in Cuba. US$1.5 million was invested in telecommunications by Mexico's, Grupo Domos.

A large part of the Cuban bureaucracy is prepared to support capitalist restoration should an accommodation with imperialism prove to be possible. The pressure for more pro-capitalist measures is set to increase. Cuba cannot exist in international isolation for an indefinite period of time and it will be forced to try and attract more foreign investment and trade. Castro and sections of the bureaucracy would probably be content to try and sustain a hybrid regime if this is possible. This would include a big element of the private market with some state ownership and planning with his state machine left in tact.

Those sections of the leadership which are more inclined towards capitalist restoration are likely to be more assertive with the death of Castro who, at 71, is in ailing health.

With a change in the Cuban leadership after Castro's death, even US imperialism could change its policy and try to incorporate a new and younger generation from the bureaucracy with the Cuban capitalist class in exile. Some sections of the ruling class in the US are already looking at this possibility and have even carried out investments in Cuba.

This was curtailed in the run-up to the last US Presidential elections as Bill Clinton tightened the embargo in part in an attempt to win the Cuban vote in Florida. However, whilst such actions may emerge as the main plank of policy even

Sugercane workers, Cuba, 1988

this would have to overcome the hatred and bitterness amongst the Cuban masses towards US imperialism and the reactionary Cuban capitalists residing in Florida. It will not be an easy journey given the conflicting interests which exist.

For a Socialist Alternative

The absence of a socialist alternative and Cuba's isolation will force the process of capitalist restoration to accelerate further. This could only be averted by establishing a regime of genuine workers' democracy, with a perspective of developing the socialist revolution throughout Latin America and internationally.

The establishment of genuine workers' councils, locally and nationally, which have control and management of the economy is essential. All representatives and officials must be elected, be subject to recall by those they represent and receive only the average wage of a skilled worker.

There must be an ending of the one-party regime which exists. This is often justified because of the threat to the revolution from imperialism and the prospect of reactionary right-wing gangs from Miami being allowed to organise their forces. This threat is real but will not be averted by only allowing the party of the bureaucracy to organise itself. All parties which are opposed to imperialism and defend the idea of a socialist planned economy should be allowed to organise, conduct propaganda and stand candidates in elections. Independent trade unions need to be established.

The threat posed by imperialism and capitalist restoration in Cuba can only be avoided through the victory of the socialist revolution throughout Latin America and internationally. For this it is necessary to win the support of the working class in Latin America and establish a socialist federation of the continent. This was necessary when Che and the revolution triumphed in 1959.

Che aspired to achieving this victory. However, despite his heroism and revolutionary sacrifice, he failed to understand how to accomplish continental socialism. Thirty years after his death this struggle is more necessary than ever. If the lessons of Che's legacy are grasped by revolutionaries internationally it will be won.

other titles available from socialist books

● **A Socialist World is Possible - The History of the CWI**
by Peter Taaffe
Published August 2004. 96 pages paperback
A balance sheet of the role, activity and contribution of the CWI to the workers'
movement internationally in the thirty years since its formation in April 1974.
Price £5.00

● **Socialists and the Venezuelan Revolution**
by Tony Saunois
Published June 2004. 68 pages paperback
On the response of revolutionaries to the revolutionary crisis in Venezuela
and the left-populist regime of President Hugo Chavez. Price £2.00

● **Empire Defeated - Vietnam War: the lessons for today**
by Peter Taaffe
Published February 2004. 128 pages paperback
A history of the Vietnam War drawing out the lessons to be learnt from this conflict,
especially in the aftermath of the Iraq war. Price £6.00

● **Socialism in the 21st Century: the way forward for anti-capitalism**
by Hannah Sell
Published August 2002. 90 pages paperback
An essential read for anti-capitalists, trade union activists and socialists. Price £5.00

● **The Rise of Militant: Militant's 30 years** by Peter Taaffe
Published 1995. 570 pages paperback
Story of Militant, forerunner of the Socialist Party (English and Welsh section
of the CWI), from its birth. Price £10.99

● **Liverpool - A city that Dared to Fight** by Tony Mulhearn and Peter Taaffe
Published 1988, 500 pages paperback
Militant led Liverpool city council's battle against the Thatcher government
1983-1997. Price £7.95

● **Cuba: Socialism and Democracy Debates on the Revolution and Cuba Today**
by Peter Taaffe
Published 2000. 120 pages paperback
Defence of the Socialist Party's analysis of the Cuban revolution. Price £5.00

the committee for a workers international

The CWI has affiliated parties and organisations in more than 35 countries on all continents. The way to contact our comrades differs from country to country. Some you can contact directly (see next page). For others, it is easier to do it via the CWI offices in London. E-mail to the International Office of the CWI: cwi@ worldsoc.co.uk or contact us at PO Box 3688, London, E11 1YE, UK. Telephone: ++ 44 (0)20 8558 5814. Fax: ++ 44 (0)20 8988 8793.

For more information on any of the issues mentioned, and to follow CWI campaigns and activities, visit the CWI website:

www.socialistworld.net

Sections in German, English, Spanish, French, Italian, Dutch, Polish, Portuguese, Swedish and Turkish

contacting the CWI

If you want to know more about the CWI in Cyprus, Finland, Ghana, Kashmir, Luxembourg, Spain or anywhere else... then contact the CWI international offices in London.
e-mail: cwi@worldsoc.co.uk or contact us at PO Box 3688, London, Ell 1YE, Britain.
Telephone: + 44 (0)20 8988 8760. Fax: + 44 (0)20 8988 8793.

Australia: Socialist Party
PO Box 1015, Collingwood, Victoria 3066
phone: + 61 3 9650 0160
e-mail: info@socialistpartyaustralia.org
Austria: Sozialistische Linkspartei
Kaiserstrasse 14/11, 1070 Wien
phone: + 43 1 524 6310
fax: + 43 1 524 6311 e-mail: slp@slp.at
Belgium: LSP/MAS PO Box 10, 1190 Vorst 3,
phone: + 32 2 345 6181
e-mail: lspmas@skynet.be
Brazil: Socialismo Revolucionario
Caixa Postal 02009, CEP 01064-970
Sao Paulo S.P. Brazil
phone: + 55 11 339 5584
e-mail: sr-cio@uol.com.br
Canada: Socialist Alternative
903-633 Bay Street, Toronto, Ontario MSG 2G4
e-mail: socialist@ canada.com
Chile: Socialismo Revolucionario
Celso C Campos, Cassilla 50310, Correo
Central, Santiago phone: + 56 2 622 9004
e-mail: jandresvena@hotmail.com
CIS 125167 Moscow a\Ya 37, Moscow, Russia
e-mail: pabgem@online.ru
**Czech Republic: Socialistická Alternativa
Budoucnost** D.V.S., PO Box 227, Bubesnké
nábfieêi 306, 170 05 Praha 7 - Hole_ovice
e-mail: budoucnost@email.cz
England & Wales: Socialist Party
PO Box 24697, London E11 1YD
phone: + 44 20 8988 8777
fax: + 44 20 8988 8787
e-mail: campaigns@socialistparty.org.uk
**France: Gauche révolutionnaire
Les amis de l'Egalite**
Centre 166, 82 rue Jeanne d' Arc, 76000 Rouen
e-mail: grcontact@hotmail.com
Germany: Sozialistische Alternative
Litten Strasse 106/107, 10179 Berlin
phone: + 49 30 2472 3802
e-mail: info@sav-online.de
Greece: Xekinima 8 Gortynos Street, PO Box
11254, Athens phone/fax: + 30 210 228 3018
e-mail: xekinima@hotmail.com
India: Dudiyora Horaata
PO Box 1828, Bangalore 560018
e-mail: newsocialist@dataone.in

Ireland North: Socialist Party
15 Lombard Street, Belfast BT1 1RB
phone: + 44 2890 232962
fax: + 44 2890 311778
e-mail: socialistpartyni@btconnect.com
Ireland South: Socialist Party PO Box 3434,
Dublin 8 phone/fax: + 353 1 677 25 92
e-mail: info@socialistparty.net
Israel: Maavak Sotzialisti
P.O.Box. 1219, Ramet Hasharon, 47111, Israel
e-mail: feedback@maavak.org.il
Italy: Lotta per il Socialismo
e-mail: lottaperilsoc@hotmail.com
Japan: Kokusai Rentai Kanayamachi Biru 3F
Kita-ku, Temma 2-1-17, Osaka-shi 530-0043
e-mail: kokusairentai@hotmail.com
Netherlands: Offensief PO Box 11561, 1001 GN
Amsterdam e-mail: info@offensief.nl
New Zealand: Socialist Alternative
e-mail: socialist_alternative@hotmail.com
Nigeria: Democratic Socialist Movement
PO Box 2225, Agege, Lagos
phone: +234 1 804 6603
e-mail: dsmcentre@hotmail.com
Pakistan: Socialist Movement Pakistan
e-mail:revolutionary1917@yahoo.com
Poland: Grupa na rzecz Parti Robotniczej (GPR)
e-mail brasio@poczta.onet.pl
Portugal: Alternativa Socialista
Apartado 27018, 1201-950, Lisboa
e-mail: alternativa.socialista@netvisao.pt
Scotland: International Socialists PO Box 6773,
Dundee DD1 IYL phone: + 44 1382 833 759
e-mail: cwi@blueyonder.co.uk
South Africa: Democratic Socialist Movement
PO Box 596, Newton, 2113 Johannesburg
phone: + 27 11 342 2220
e-mail: democraticsocialist@mweb.co.za
Sri Lanka: United Socialist Party
261/1 Kirula Road, Narahenpito, Colombo 5
phone: + 94 1 508 821 e-mail: usp@wow.lk
Sweden: Rattvisepartiet Socialisterna
PO Box 73, 123 03 Farsta
phone: + 46 8 605 9400 fax: + 46 8 556 252 52
e-mail: rs@socialisterna.org
USA: Socialist Alternative
PO Box 45343, Seattle W4 98145
e-mail: info@socialistalternative.org